Assessing Quality in Postsecondary Education

International Perspectives

Edited by

HARVEY P. WEINGARTEN, MARTIN HICKS,
and AMY KAUFMAN

Queen's Policy Studies Series
School of Policy Studies, Queen's University
McGill-Queen's University Press
Montréal & Kingston | London | Ithaca

Queen's | Policy Studies

School of Policy Studies Publications Program
Robert Sutherland Hall
138 Union Street
Kingston, ON K7L 3N6
www.queensu.ca/sps/

Library and Archives Canada Cataloguing in Publication

Assessing quality in postsecondary education : international perspectives
/ edited by Harvey P. Weingarten, Martin Hicks, and Amy Kaufman.

(Queen's policy studies series)
Issued in print and electronic formats.
ISBN 978-1-55339-532-4 (softcover).--ISBN 978-1-55339-533-1 (PDF).--
ISBN 978-1-55339-534-8 (HTML)

1. Universities and colleges--Evaluation--Case studies. 2. Universities and colleges--Standards--Case studies. 3. Total quality management in higher education--Case studies. I. Weingarten, Harvey P., 1952-, editor II. Hicks, Martin, 1957-, editor III. Kaufman, Amy, 1977-, editor IV. Series: Queen's policy studies series

LB2331.62.A87 2018   378.01   C2018-900917-9
                                              C2018-900918-7

Table of Contents

Section II: Europe

Section III: Canada

Section IV: The Future of Quality Measurement

Chapter 10

Hamish Coates

Harvey P. Weingarten, Martin Hicks, and Amy Kaufman

About the Authors

Roger Benjamin has been president and CEO of the Council for Aid to Education since 2005. Prior to the appointment, he was a research scientist at the RAND Corporation and director of RAND Education. He has also served as provost at the University of Minnesota, provost and senior vice-chancellor at the University of Pittsburgh, and as a professor of political science at both institutions.

Hamish Coates is a tenured professor at Tsinghua University's Institute of Education, and also deputy director of its Centre for the Assessment of College and Student Development. He previously held positions as a professor of higher education at the University of Melbourne, founding director of higher education research at the Australian Council for Educational Research, and program director at the LH Martin Institute for Tertiary Leadership and Management. He concentrates on improving the quality and productivity of higher education.

Fergal Costello was head of system performance and development at the Higher Education Authority (HEA) in Ireland, where he headed the development of new performance compacts with higher-education institutions. He joined Ireland's Department of Education and Science in 1995 and previously worked in the Department of Finance and, since 2001, at the HEA. He has performed a number of different roles including head of policy and planning, and head of funding (Institutes of Technology). He recently took a position in the newly formed Government Department of Rural and Community Development.

Ava Czapalay is senior executive director of the Nova Scotia Department of Labour and Advanced Education. She serves on the board of the Maritime Provinces Higher Education Commission, and the Council of Atlantic Ministers of Education and Training, and is the chair of the Postsecondary Education Working Committee of the Council of

Ministers of Education, Canada. Previously, she was a corporate strategist with the Nova Scotia Department of Economic and Rural Development, and the founding president and CEO of EduNova.

Ellen Hazelkorn is a professor emeritus, director of the higher-education policy research unit at the Dublin Institute of Technology, and an education consultant with BH Associates. She is joint editor of *Policy Reviews in Higher Education*, international co-investigator at the ESRC/HEFCE Centre for Global Higher Education, and research fellow at the Center for International Higher Education at Boston College. She was a policy adviser to, and a board member of, Ireland's Higher Education Authority, and president of the European Society for Higher Education.

Martin Hicks is executive director of data, statistics, and evaluation at the Higher Education Quality Council of Ontario (HEQCO). He is responsible for building HEQCO's data infrastructure and capacity. Previously, he served in the Ontario Cabinet Office and as a senior administrator at Durham College. He received his BA and LLB from the University of Toronto.

Aaron S. Horn is director for policy research at the Midwestern Higher Education Compact (MHEC). He leads research initiatives intended to inform state policy making and institutional practice in such areas as performance evaluation, academic preparation, and college affordability. He also co-directs a regional effort to advance environmental sustainability in higher education. Prior to joining MHEC, he conducted educational research at the University of Minnesota on topics including internationalization, youth volunteerism, and the long-term impact of study abroad on global civic engagement.

Amy Kaufman is director of special projects at the Higher Education Quality Council of Ontario. She previously worked in strategic planning and government relations in the Ontario college sector. She holds an MA in Political Science from the University of Toronto and a BA from the University of Guelph.

Roger King is chair of governors of the UK College of Business and Computing, visiting professor at the School of Management at the University of Bath, and research associate at the Centre for the Analysis of Risk and Regulation at the London School of Economics and Political Science. He co-chaired the Higher Education Commission's inquiry into regulation, was vice-chancellor of the University of Lincoln from

1996–2001, and founding chair of the Institute for Learning and Teaching in Higher Education (now the Higher Education Academy) from 1998–2001.

Jillian Kinzie is associate director of the Center for Postsecondary Research and the National Survey of Student Engagement (NSSE) Institute, where she conducts research and leads project activities on the effective use of student-engagement data to improve educational quality. She also serves as senior scholar for the National Institute for Learning Outcomes Assessment project. Prior to her tenure at NSSE, she coordinated the master's program in Higher Education and Student Affairs at Indiana University. She has more than a decade of additional experience as a research associate, and in leadership roles in academic and student affairs.

Maureen Mancuso is a professor in the Department of Political Science at the University of Guelph, where she formerly served as provost and vice-president, academic. She is a policy fellow at the Council of Ontario Universities (COU), and serves as chair of the COU Task Force on Quality Indicators.

Alexander C. McCormick is director of the National Survey of Student Engagement and holds a faculty appointment in the Educational Leadership and Policy Studies Department at the Indiana University School of Education, where he teaches in the Higher Education and Student Affairs program. Prior to joining Indiana University, he served as senior scholar at the Carnegie Foundation for the Advancement of Teaching.

Duff Montgomerie was appointed deputy minister of the Nova Scotia Department of Labour and Advanced Education in 2014. Prior to the appointment, he served as deputy minister in the Departments of Natural Resources, and Health Promotion and Protection. He has also chaired the Premier's Council on Canadian Health Awareness, served as director of community relations for the Premier's Office, and a senior policy adviser at the Treasury and Policy Board.

Cláudia S. Sarrico is the lead policy analyst for the Benchmarking Higher Education System Performance project of the Directorate for Education and Skills at the OECD. Previously she was an associate professor at ISEG Lisbon School of Economics and Management, and senior researcher with CIPES Centre for Research in Higher Education Policies, where she led research on resources, performance, and human capital. She has held a number of policy advisory positions with the Portuguese Ministry of Education and Science, Foundation for Science and Technology, and the Agency for the Assessment and Accreditation of Higher Education.

Jeremy Smith is the director of policy and planning for the Nova Scotia Department of Education and Early Childhood Development. He oversees the development and review of policies related to the delivery of public education in the province of Nova Scotia, and is responsible for overseeing both legislative and regulatory amendments related to the mandate of the Department of Education and Early Childhood Development.

David A. Tandberg is vice-president of policy research and strategic initiatives at the State Higher Education Executive Officers (SHEEO), where he evaluates state policies meant to increase student access and success in higher education. He serves as an associate editor of *Educational Researcher* and is on the editorial boards of *The Journal of Higher Education* and *The Journal of Education Finance*. Prior to his tenure at SHEEO, he was an associate professor of higher education and associate director of the Center for Postsecondary Success at Florida State University. He also served as a special assistant to the secretary of education in the Pennsylvania Department of Education.

Frans van Vught is a high-level expert and adviser at the European Commission. He has chaired groups on various EU policies in the fields of innovation, higher education, and research. He has served as president and rector magnificus at the University of Twente in the Netherlands, and has been president of various European higher-education organizations. He has an honorary professorial chair at the University of Twente, is an honorary professional fellow at the University of Melbourne, and holds several honorary doctorates. He is one of two leaders of the EU-sponsored project on the development of a new, multi-dimensional, and user-driven global ranking tool called U-Multirank.

Harvey P. Weingarten is president and CEO of the Higher Education Quality Council of Ontario, an independent agency of the Ontario government with the legislated mandate to improve the accessibility, quality, and accountability of the province's colleges and universities. He formerly served as president and vice-chancellor at the University of Calgary, and provost at McMaster University.

Introduction

Harvey P. Weingarten, Martin Hicks, and Amy Kaufman

Universities and colleges find themselves under mounting pressure to measure their performance. Some of this stems from an increasing public and government desire to hold higher-education institutions accountable for their use of public funds. More generally, all stakeholders, but particularly students and governments, are asking questions about the value they derive from their investment of money (and time) in higher education. At the loftiest level, this demand for performance measurement reflects a recognition that the outputs of postsecondary institutions—the highly educated students they graduate, the research and innovation they spawn, and the communities they support—are essential to a robust and vibrant society that is competitive economically, and that sustains a high quality of life.

As a result, colleges and universities are subject to an increasing reporting burden. They report on everything from enrolments (often counted in different ways for different purposes for different audiences), to staff numbers, faculty awards and prizes, capital spending, the condition of their infrastructure, degrees awarded, debt and loans, salaries and benefits, fundraising and endowments, and student services. Yet, despite the fact that they are first and foremost institutions of higher learning, colleges and universities seldom report on what, or how well, their students have learned.

As an agency of the Ontario government, the Higher Education Quality Council of Ontario (HEQCO) has a legislated mandate to, among other things, evaluate the province's postsecondary education sector and report the results to the minister and the public. We have previously published several assessments of the Canadian and Ontario postsecondary systems and we are in the process of developing a contemporary and dynamic dashboard to continually monitor the changes in, and the performance of, the Ontario system.

Some aspects of performance—such as access, enrolments, finances, and research—are reasonably easy to measure and there are acknowledged indicators used to do so. But these measures overlook what is most important: how well institutions teach and students learn, and the overall quality of the student experience. These should be at the very heart of any instrument that purports to evaluate and measure higher education. As we have argued previously, it is inconceivable from our perspective to measure the performance of a postsecondary system without having measures of academic quality—what and how well students learn—at its core.

But how does one measure what students learn or the academic quality of a college or university? To some, measuring academic quality is akin to US Supreme Court Justice Potter Stewart's famous quip about defining pornography: "I know it when I see it." But this falls far short of any rigorous performance-measurement regime or attempt to monitor how the quality of institutions and the system may be changing.

Fortunately, we are not alone in grappling with this challenge. To better understand how others are attempting to measure academic quality, we convened a two-day workshop in May 2017 to learn from a group of experts from around the world who are working on this problem. We deliberately selected participants who have adopted different approaches to the issue—from the use of quality surrogate measures such as student satisfaction and graduation rates, to direct measures of critical-thinking skills using standardized tests, and inventories of multiple measures embedded in national reporting schemes. Workshop participants from Australia, Ireland, the United States, the Netherlands, Canada, the United Kingdom, and the Organisation for Economic Co-operation and Development (OECD) were asked to provide their perspectives, experiences, insights, and opinions on several questions:

1. What aspects of postsecondary academic quality, student learning, and the educational experience do you feel are the most important to measure or give the best insight into these issues?

2. Specifically, how are you currently measuring or planning to mea-

sure these attributes? What specific indicators or measures do you recommend and why?

3. How are, or should, these measures be used by institutions and governments (or bodies associated with government such as quality-assurance boards and accreditation bodies)? How are these measures reported and disseminated, and what impact have they had on curricula, policy development, and resource allocation by governments and institutions?

Workshop participants did not disappoint us. From Frans van Vught; Duff Montgomerie, Ava Czapalay and Jeremy Smith; Maureen Mancuso; and Ellen Hazelkorn and Fergal Costello, we learned how the measurement of quality was inextricably linked to government attempts to hold their higher-education systems accountable for the use of public funds and the improvement of the quality of the student experience. From Roger King we learned about perhaps the most ambitious experiment underway: the UK's Teaching Excellence and Student Outcomes Framework. We learned about broad, comprehensive approaches to monitoring almost all aspects of a higher-education institution's function (of which quality issues were but one component), best exemplified by Cláudia Sarrico's presentation on the OECD's benchmarking approach. And we heard about attempts to use standardized, psychometrically validated tools—best exemplified in a presentation by Roger Benjamin—to provide direct measures of the degree to which a postsecondary education enhanced the acquisition of cognitive skills, such as critical thinking.

Contributions by Aaron Horn and David Tandberg, and by Jillian Kinzie and Alexander McCormick provided excellent analyses of the considerations that should go into the selection of quality indicators, and appropriate cautions about the potential unintended and undesired consequences. We heard warnings of how attempts to measure quality can inadvertently increase institutional selectivity at the expense of access, lead to institutional conformity, and raise concerns over institutional autonomy. The following chapters, which we have grouped geographically, expand on these distinct approaches, ideas, and perspectives.

We end with Hamish Coates who provides a new and contemporary way to think about the quality question that is more relevant to governments and the public; specifically, by talking about the value of going to a postsecondary institution.

As we had hoped, the presentations sharpened our thinking about how to measure academic quality and led us to definitive conclusions about how we would do so as we develop instruments to measure the academic quality of the Ontario system. Our conclusions are presented in the final chapter of the book.

Abbreviations

AAC&U	Association of American Colleges and Universities
AHELO	Assessment of Higher Education Learning Outcomes
AUSSE	Australasian Survey of Student Engagement
CAE	Council for Aid to Education
CLA	Collegiate Learning Assessment
CLA+	Collegiate Learning Assessment Plus
DQP	Degree Qualifications Profile
EASI	Essential Adult Skills Initiative
EIs	engagement indicators
EIA	Excellence in Assessment
ES	effect size
ETP	Effective Teaching Practices
HEA	Higher Education Authority
HEFCE	Higher Education Funding Council for England
HEQCO	Higher Education Quality Council of Ontario
HIPs	high-impact practices

HLC	Higher Learning Commission
INES	Indicators of Education Systems
IoTs	institutes of technology
ISSE	Irish Survey of Student Engagement
KPI	key performance indicator
MAESD	Ministry of Advanced Education and Skills Development
MCL	Measuring College Learning
MPHEC	Maritime Provinces Higher Education Commission
MSC	Multi-State Collaborative to Advance Student Learning
MYAA	Multi-Year Accountability Agreement
NAEP	National Assessment of Educational Progress
NILOA	National Institute for Learning Outcomes Assessment
NSCAD	Nova Scotia College of Art and Design
NSCC	Nova Scotia Community College
NSS	National Student Survey
NSSE	National Survey of Student Engagement
OCAV	Ontario Council of Academic Vice-presidents
OFFA	Office for Fair Access
PBL	problem-based learning
PIAAC	Program for the International Assessment of Adult Competencies
PISA	Programme for International Student Assessment
QAA	Quality Assurance Agency
REF	Research Excellence Framework
RTC	Regional Technical Colleges
SFI	Science Foundation Ireland
SMA	Strategic Mandate Agreement

TALIS	Teaching and Learning International Survey
TEF	Teaching Excellence and Student Outcomes Framework
UAS	universities of applied sciences
UDLEs	undergraduate degree-level expectations
VALUE	Valid Assessment of Learning in Undergraduate Education

Section I

The United States

1

Indicators of Educational Quality for Postsecondary Accountability Systems

Aaron S. Horn and David A. Tandberg

The United States is widely revered for its presumed excellence in higher education, and it now seems commonplace to characterize our postsecondary system as "the envy of the world" (e.g., Khator 2011). In fact, according to the Academic Ranking of World Universities—which heavily weights research productivity—fifty of the top 100 universities globally reside in the United States (Shanghai Ranking Consultancy 2016). Few informed observers, however, would equate research prowess with educational effectiveness. Indeed, the educational quality of postsecondary institutions has been increasingly called into question as evidence periodically surfaces of marginal knowledge and skill acquisition among college graduates (Arum and Roska 2011; Kutner et al. 2007; Desjardins et al. 2013). For example, results from the National Assessment of Adult Literacy indicated that only 40 percent of bachelor's degree recipients were proficient in prose literacy in 1992, a figure that fell to 31 percent in 2003 (Kutner et al. 2007). More recently, a national survey revealed that only 24 percent of employers agreed that college graduates were well prepared for "applying knowledge/skills to [the] real world" (Hart Research Associates 2015, 12).

Concerns about educational quality have also emerged amidst competing state budgetary priorities and low graduation rates, as colleges and universities are pressured to provide evidence of their value, effectiveness, and efficiency, thereby ensuring that taxpayer investments

Assessing Quality in Postsecondary Education: International Perspectives, edited by Harvey P. Weingarten, Martin Hicks, and Amy Kaufman. Montréal and Kingston: McGill-Queen's University Press, Queen's Policy Studies Series. © 2018 The School of Policy Studies, Queen's University at Kingston. All rights reserved.

in higher education are being utilized responsibly. Policy makers have thus issued a clarion call for greater accountability related to educational quality in the postsecondary sector, particularly the need to collect and publicize data on student learning outcomes (e.g., Reindl and Reyna 2011; SHEEO 2005; US Department of Education 2006). This chapter seeks to inform policy discourse by providing an overview of performance indicators used to evaluate educational quality for purposes of public accountability and improvement in higher education.

Toward Which End?

If the old adage that *whatever is measured is valued* holds true, a comprehensive conception of the aims of higher education must remain at the fore to ensure that stakeholders understand not only what is valued in student learning, but more importantly, what is not. While the public is generally aware that colleges should promote degree completion to the extent possible, few students enter (or leave) college with an understanding of what should be learned. Nonetheless, much ink has been spilled over attempts to delineate essential learning outcomes, frequently with remarkable commonalities across frameworks (e.g., AAC&U 2007; Adelman et al. 2014; Markle et al. 2013). Three national initiatives to establish norms for student learning outcomes are noteworthy. In its report, *College Learning for the New Global Century*, the Association of American Colleges and Universities (2007) outlined a set of student outcomes that were endorsed by a panel of diverse leaders representing the education, business, non-profit, and government sectors. The panel sought to identify the critical competencies for life, work, and citizenship that should be expected of all college graduates, regardless of degree level or institution type. The resulting learning outcomes were subsumed within four rubrics: (a) knowledge of human cultures and the physical and natural world; (b) intellectual and practical skills; (c) personal and social responsibility; and (d) integrative and applied learning (see Table 1.1).

In another prominent example, the Lumina Foundation's Degree Qualifications Profile (DQP) provided a similar conceptual framework for learning outcomes: specialized knowledge, broad and integrative knowledge, intellectual skills, applied and collaborative learning, and civic and global learning (Adelman et al. 2014). Moreover, the DQP extended previous work by specifying levels of proficiency for each outcome by degree level (i.e., associate, bachelor's, master's). Finally,

Table 1.1

AAC&U's Ideal Learning Outcomes

Outcome Rubric	Defining Elements
Knowledge of Human Cultures and the Physical and Natural World	Through study in the sciences and mathematics, social sciences, humanities, histories, languages, and the arts
Intellectual and Practical Skills	Inquiry and analysis Critical and creative thinking Written and oral communication Quantitative literacy Information literacy Teamwork and problem solving
Personal and Social Responsibility	Civic knowledge and engagement—local and global Intercultural knowledge and competence Ethical reasoning and action Foundations and skills for lifelong learning
Integrative and Applied Learning	Synthesis and advanced accomplishment across general and specialized studies

Source: Adapted from *College Learning for the New Global Century* by the Association of American Colleges and Universities (2007).

whereas the aforementioned initiatives mainly focused on learning outcomes applicable to all college graduates, the Social Science Research Council led a two-year project, Measuring College Learning (MCL), to facilitate faculty discourse on disciplinary learning outcomes (Arum, Roska, and Cook 2016). The MCL project engaged faculty in biology, history, economics, communication, sociology, and business.

Defining Educational Quality

Numerous competing definitions of quality have been used, implicitly or explicitly, in the field of higher education with varying emphases on inputs, processes, and outcomes (Harvey and Green 1993; Campbell 2015). The resources and reputation model is the oldest approach, for example, and equates quality with prestige and inputs. This model is readily observed in nearly every ranking system produced for popular consumption, such as *US News and World Report's Best Colleges*, which evaluates institutions based on class size, faculty salary, admissions test scores, per-student expenditures, and other factors. A major problem with this approach is that the presence of impressive resources and a strong reputation among peers do not permit inferences about effective resource utilization and learning outcomes, which are central concerns in the context of public accountability. Research has long revealed only modest relationships between traditional input measures and learning gains in college (Mayhew et al. 2016), thereby preserving the etymological roots of prestige in the Latin *praestīgiae*, or juggler's tricks.

The working definition of quality in this chapter, therefore, focuses less on inputs and more on educational practices and student outcomes, namely the extent to which an institution meets reasonable standards in (a) employing programs, practices, and policies that are generally known to be conducive to student learning and timely degree completion; (b) enabling and adding value to student outcomes; and (c) ensuring that graduates have fulfilled learning objectives. These dimensions of educational practice, institutional effectiveness, and degree integrity, along with exemplary performance indicators, are elaborated below.

Good Educational Practice

Educational practice indicators have rarely been considered within state accountability systems based on the principle that institutions should retain autonomy over the design of the curriculum, pedagogy, and support services. However, this objection withers with the realization that the amount of autonomy ceded will be contingent on the level of practice specification and the type of accountability system. For instance, the specification of a good pedagogical practice such as "giving useful feedback" is sufficiently abstract to permit a myriad of qualifying faculty behaviours; there is no standard response X prescribed in classroom situation A. Moreover, a process orientation to educational quality is complementary insofar as it offers some accountability-related advantages over outcome-based assessment approaches. Whereas an institution can assume responsibility for educational practices, student-learning outcomes are partly a function of factors that frequently lie beyond institutional control, particularly student academic aptitude, preparation, and motivation (e.g., Liu, Bridgeman, and Adler 2012). Even when such extraneous influences are parsed out of the outcome in the form of an adjusted gain score, institutional leaders and faculty are left with little actionable knowledge for improvement. Conversely, an accountability system that incorporates process measures creates stronger expectations and clearer feedback for shaping faculty and staff behaviour. Finally, a central rationale for directly evaluating educational practice is the difficulty in adequately assessing the full range of ideal learning outcomes due to constraints in resources and the availability of appropriate measures. It is much easier to determine whether a putative best practice is prevalent than to ascertain its intended effect.

The identification of good educational practices should be based on expert consensus and empirical linkages with desirable student outcomes. Accordingly, this section draws on past conceptions of good practices that have been associated with academic engagement, learning, and persistence outcomes (e.g. Ewell and Jones 1996; Jankowski 2017; Kuh et al. 2011; Kuh, 2008; National Research Council 2013; Tinto 2012). For instance, among the most influential frameworks, Kuh et al. (2011) argued that highly effective institutions can be distinguished by their level of academic challenge, use of active and collaborative learning, student-faculty interaction, student involvement in enriching educational experiences, and a supportive campus environment. Kuh's framework has gained national prominence through the administration of the National Survey of Student Engagement, or NSSE (McCormick, Kinzie, and Gonyea 2013). Although far from perfect, the NSSE currently provides the best balance among key test selection criteria, specifically the cost of administration, the ease of analysis and interpretation, widespread adoption, and reliability and validity. In fact, the NSSE scales have been recently used as educational practice indicators for public accountability in Maine, Tennessee, Vermont, Wisconsin, and Wyoming. However, rather than simply convert the entire set of NSSE items into performance measures, we recommend a subset of four practice indicators that have garnered the strongest support in empirical studies: (1) instructional excellence, (2) highly effective programs, (3) academic challenge, and (4) academic and social support.

Indicator 1: Instructional Excellence

The first indicator assesses the extent to which faculty are using effective instructional techniques. For example, the National Research Council (2013) reviewed research in educational psychology and identified several pedagogical practices that are conducive to deep learning,[1] such

---

1 Deep (or deeper) learning refers to meaningful learning that promotes both retention and transfer of knowledge to novel situations (Mayer, 2011).

as representing concepts in multiple modes; using examples, cases, and models; and providing formative assessments that improve the learning process. More generally, after controlling for student background characteristics, researchers found that the presentation of a course in an organized and well-planned manner was positively associated with gains on standardized tests of reading comprehension (Bray, Pascarella, and Pierson 2004) and critical thinking (Loes, Salisbury, and Pascarella 2015) as well as the likelihood of student persistence (Pascarella, Salisbury, and Blaich 2011). This research provides a satisfactory basis for measuring instructional excellence with the NSSE Effective Teaching Practices (ETP) scale, wherein students report whether their professors used examples to explain difficult concepts; taught courses in an organized way; and gave timely and useful feedback, among other techniques. The ETP scale has been positively associated with self-reported learning gains during the first year of college (Zilvinskis, Masseria, and Pike 2017).

Indicator 2: Highly Effective Programs

Highly effective programs refer to structured curricular and co-curricular activities that are grounded in sound pedagogical principles and have been demonstrated to reliably yield intended learning outcomes. Kuh (2008) identified an extensive array of "high-impact practices" that have been consistently associated with self-reported learning gains including participation in a learning community, service learning, research with faculty, internships, study abroad, and senior-year capstone courses or projects. Kuh argued that such experiences tend to demand a high degree of student effort, promote faculty and peer interactions, expose students to diverse ideas and people, incite feedback from others, and require the application and integration of knowledge. However, empirical support varies considerably for these practices, and resource constraints may prevent broad diffusion in some cases, particularly providing opportunities for students to conduct research with faculty. A further limitation of the NSSE high-impact practice index is the omission of other effective pedagogical models.

Whereas evidence is generally supportive for learning communities (Weiss et al. 2015), living-learning programs (Inkelas and Soldner 2011), study abroad (Horn and Fry 2013), and internships (Reddy and Moores 2012), less is known about the impact of culminating senior experiences. In contrast, a rather robust corpus of research has demonstrated the effectiveness of community service and service learning in both secondary and postsecondary sectors (Horn 2012; Yorio and Ye 2012). Yorio and Ye (2012) conducted a meta-analysis of forty studies that examined service learning during college in relation to cognitive development (e.g., GPA, course performance, problem solving) and found an average effect size (ES) of .53, or a difference of 20 percentile points. Other meta-analyses have estimated the effect size to be closer to .31 (Celio, Durlak, and Dymnicki 2011; Warren, 2012).

Absent from Kuh's (2008) initial list are other pedagogical models with strong empirical support, including problem-based learning and co-operative learning. Problem-based learning (PBL) is a student-centred pedagogy, which uses representative problems that organize and stimulate the learning experience (Barrows 1996). In their meta-analysis of forty-three studies, Dochy et al. (2003) found that PBL was associated with significant gains in the ability to apply knowledge (ES = .66; 25 percentile points) relative to the traditional lecture method. Collaborative or co-operative learning involves small groups of students (typically two to four per group) who collaborate in a specific way to attain a common learning goal.[2] Meta-analyses have provided overwhelming support in favour of co-operative learning relative to traditional individual or competitive learning (Johnson, Johnson, and Smith 1998; Kyndt et al. 2013). Academic achievement gains approximate an effect size of .49 to .53, or 19 to 20 percentile points. The diffusion of such pedagogical models remains one of the most urgent priorities in higher education as 51 percent of faculty at four-year institutions principally employ "extensive lecturing" in most of their courses (Eagan et al. 2014).

Indicator 3: Academic Challenge

The academic challenge indicator evaluates the rigour of the college curriculum, especially whether learning activities emphasize conceptual depth and integration rather than the simple reproduction of course material (Biggs and Tang 2011; Campbell and Cabrera 2014). To be sure, in contradistinction to the metaphor of students as empty vessels that

---

2 In co-operative learning, the instructor ensures that (a) individual performance is intertwined with group performance; (b) each student is held accountable for his or her performance; (c) students enhance each other's learning outcomes through explanations, modelling, reinforcement, and coaching; (d) students develop requisite social skills for effective teamwork; and (e) students evaluate and improve group work processes (Johnson, Johnson, and Smith 1998).

must be relentlessly filled with facts, educational psychologists have demonstrated that students learn by actively constructing knowledge through the explanation, application, and integration of new concepts (Barkley 2009). Academic challenges of this sort can be assessed through the NSSE Reflective and Integrative Learning scale, wherein students are asked about whether they were able to connect topics across courses; link classroom learning with community problems; and connect new course material to prior knowledge, *inter alia*. Student scores on this scale have been associated with gains in critical-thinking skills, the need for cognition, and a positive attitude toward literacy (Nelson Laird et al. 2014).

Indicator 4: Academic and Social Support

The final practice indicator evaluates the effectiveness of the institution's academic and social support. Past research has revealed that a variety of academic support programs can promote student persistence, such as first-year seminars, student success courses, tutoring, and summer bridge programs (Asmussen and Horn 2014). Effective support also involves providing opportunities for social integration (Tinto 2012) and promoting psychological welfare (Francis and Horn 2017). Pertinent items in NSSE form the supportive environment scale, which assesses student perceptions of institutional support for academic success and meaningful campus activities, for instance. While controlling for potentially confounding student and institutional characteristics, an earlier version of the supportive environment scale predicted higher retention and graduation rates (Gordon, Ludlum, and Hoey 2008; Pike 2013).

Institutional Effectiveness

The current knowledge base of good educational practice can inform the development of relevant indicators, but a quality-assurance system must permit the evolution of practice and acknowledge the limits of our ability to precisely specify the nature of good practice. The second facet of our definition of educational quality thus regards outcome-based evidence for whether the institution is enabling and adding value to student learning and degree completion. Measures of institutional effectiveness are not intended to provide focused diagnostic feedback, but rather identify a general need for closer scrutiny of institutional practices (for remediation or emulation). Two indicators are proposed to assess added value: (a) basic skills development and (b) promoting timely completion.

Indicator 5: Basic Skills Development

Any of the learning outcomes previously outlined in Table 1.1 might be subject to assessment, but several constraints will quickly temper overly enthusiastic proposals: resources are limited, the state of test development varies, some learning outcomes enjoy greater consensus, and certain skill deficits are better documented than others. The simplest and most popular approach draws upon the self-reported (or perceived) learning gains of college seniors. For example, according to national NSSE results, the majority of students believed that their institution contributed quite a bit (38 percent) or very much (47 percent) to their critical-thinking ability (NSSE 2017). However, while a student experience survey is a low-cost solution to learning assessment, it may not be a valid one. Past research has indicated that self-reported learning gains are at best only weakly correlated with gains on standardized achievement measures (Bowman 2010, 2011; Porter 2013; Sitzmann et al. 2010). Self-reported learning gains instead appear to assess student satisfaction with the academic experience (Gonyea and Miller 2011; Sitzmann et al. 2010).

The preferred alternative to self-reported learning gains is to directly measure student learning. The most advanced testing initiatives have focused on critical thinking, writing, reading, and quantitative literacy. This partly reflects a strong consensus around these abilities among faculty at four-year institutions, wherein 99 percent believe that critical thinking is an essential or very important learning goal for all undergraduates, followed by the ability to write effectively (93 percent; Eagan et al. 2014). The ETS Proficiency Profile, the ACT CAAP, and the Council for Aid to Education's Collegiate Learning Assessment Plus (CLA+) are among the most established assessments of these basic skills. In fact, Klein, Liu, and Sconing's (2009) validation study demonstrated that institution-level scores from these three measures are highly reliable and strongly inter-correlated, though there are some important differences that should be considered before selecting a test for performance reporting.

The ETS Proficiency Profile and the ACT CAAP employ a multiple-choice format in assessing reading, writing, mathematics, and critical thinking (the CAAP also includes a science module). In support of the ETS measure, Roohr, Liu, and Liu (2016) found that the number of completed credits during college predicted critical-thinking gains. Furthermore, the ETS measure detects average gains in critical thinking (ES = .57) that are comparable to those documented in the literature using other tests for critical thinking. For instance, Huber and Kuncel's (2016) meta-analysis revealed an average gain during college of about .59 (50th to 72nd percentile). Conversely, Klein, Liu, and Sconing (2009) found that the ACT CAAP had a very wide 95 percent confidence interval for critical-thinking gains (ES = .06 to .56).

The CLA+[3] is notable for moving beyond multiple choice to so-called constructed response formats, wherein students create their own response to a prompt rather than choose from a set of predefined options. Constructed response tests appear to better ensure that students demonstrate understanding rather than simple recall. For instance, Hyytinen et al.'s (2015) analysis of responses to multiple-choice and constructed response items suggested that students with a high multiple-choice test score, but a low CLA score, had likely engaged in superficial information processing. However, it remains unclear whether the CLA+ can reliably detect gains in critical thinking, as Klein, Liu, and Sconing (2009) found that the average adjusted CLA gain score for the performance task did not significantly differ from zero.

A common objection to using standardized achievement measures is that many students may not put forth their best effort. This is a valid concern as the results of low-stakes testing are highly contingent on student motivation (Liu, Bridgeman, and Adler 2012; Finney et al. 2016). One of the few effective solutions is to raise the stakes of the test by linking it with grades or degree conferral, though this route presents several technical and political obstacles (Wise and DeMars 2005), such as faculty resistance. In another tactic, monetary incentives have been shown to increase student motivation in some cases (Duckworth et al. 2011; cf. O'Neil et al. 2005), but the cost implications arguably threaten the long-term sustainability of test administration. More promising approaches under development modify the perceived meaning and consequences of testing. Past research has indicated that motivation can be improved by ensuring that students understand the purpose of accountability testing (Zilberberg et al. 2014) and informing students that

---

3   The current version of this instrument, termed the CLA+, differs from the previous CLA in important ways. However, the core performance task for assessing critical thinking and written communication remains unchanged.

test results will affect their institution's reputation and perceptions of degree quality (Liu, Rios, and Borden 2015; cf. Kornhauser et al. 2014). However, simply notifying students that test results will provide valuable feedback for personal development or will be shared with faculty has no reliable effect on student motivation (Finney et al. 2016). Finally, in the absence of effective motivational interventions, design and statistical methods have been developed to detect unmotivated students to remove them from the sample (Swerdzewski, Harmes, and Finney 2011; Rios, Liu, and Bridgeman 2014).

Indicator 6: Promoting Timely Completion

A prominent aim of recent public accountability models has been to increase the production of postsecondary credentials. Many states have established college attainment goals in response to projected shortfalls in the supply of adults with college credentials (Lumina Foundation 2016). Moreover, high dropout rates reduce the state's return on investment through lost institutional appropriations and student grant aid as well as lost revenue from state income tax (Schneider and Yin 2011). Graduation rates have thus been adopted or proposed as a core performance indicator in state accountability systems across the US. Unfortunately, raw graduation rates are mainly a function of factors over which most institutions have very limited control, such as the academic preparedness of incoming students (e.g., Adelman 2006). While the goal of promoting student persistence is praiseworthy, drawing conclusions from raw graduation rates is a highly questionable endeavour, particularly in the context of performance funding (Horn and Lee 2017).

A potential solution lies in a value-added approach that estimates the difference between actual and predicted graduation rates (Horn and Lee 2016; Horn, Horner, and Lee 2017). In this statistical method, institutional conditions are considered to be conducive to timely completion to the extent that the actual graduation rate approximates or exceeds the rate that is predicted from student characteristics and other factors that cannot be reasonably placed under institutional control. For instance, Horn and Lee's (2016) value-added model for four-year colleges and universities accounted for institutional mission, control (public, private), and size; admissions selectivity; graduate student enrolment; student demographics (i.e., academic preparedness, gender, ethnicity, age, federal grant recipients); educational expenditures; urbanicity; and the size of the state's knowledge labour market. Their psychometric evaluation of the resulting measure demonstrated that properly specified regression models can indeed yield reliable and valid estimates of institutional effectiveness. A similar value-added completion indicator is being used for performance reporting in the City University of New York system (see McDonnell et al. 2013).

Degree Integrity

In the third dimension of educational quality, degree integrity reflects the extent to which college graduates have fulfilled learning objectives, that is, whether an institution's standards for degree conferral establish a reasonable level of concordance between actual and ideal outcomes. To be sure, perceived shortcomings in the integrity of college degrees are partly responsible for the increased scrutiny of educational quality. An increasingly popular approach among policy makers is to use employment outcomes, particularly the salary of college graduates, as proxies for skill proficiency (e.g., Sparks and Waits 2011). However, it remains unclear whether earnings constitute a defensible indicator in this regard. Studies that control for institutional selectivity, academic major, and student background characteristics, for instance, suggest that college GPA has a null or small positive effect on post-college earnings (Donhardt 2004; Zhang 2008).

Although institutions bear the ultimate responsibility for degree conferral, there are contextual contingencies that may limit an institution's performance on indicators of degree integrity, particularly a reliance on local pools of incoming students and the corresponding quality of their PK–12[4] education as well as both the economic and political consequences of depressed graduation rates resulting from unattainable academic standards. Consequently, an important caveat is that performance on degree integrity indicators is more appropriately conceived as representing the effectiveness of the PK–16 system (and beyond) rather than that of the postsecondary institution in question. While mindful of this limitation, three indicators are proposed to evaluate degree integrity: (a) basic skills proficiency, (b) major field competence, and (c) civic engagement.

---

4   PK–12 refers to preschool and kindergarten through 12th grade of secondary school. PK–16 refers to preschool and kindergarten through the completion of a four-year baccalaureate program.

Indicator 7: Basic Skills Proficiency

Whereas the metric for basic skills development assesses the value an institution adds to student learning, an indicator of basic skills *proficiency* provides the percentage of graduates who meet or exceed a performance threshold. Data collection for the former can thus be readily applied to the latter. In addition, current testing options afford an opportunity to benchmark performance beyond national borders to evaluate the competitiveness of a state's workforce in the global arena. The most widely used measure is the OECD's Program for the International Assessment of Adult Competencies (PIAAC), which assesses adult literacy, numeracy, and problem solving in technology-rich environments. The principal challenge is to control for the source of the respondent's education as cross-state migration can confound inferences of system effectiveness.

Indicator 8: Major Field Competence

Major field coursework typically occupies half of the undergraduate curriculum in the United States, and thus a corresponding performance indicator is in order. One option is to administer the ETS subject exams if they have been endorsed by faculty and professional associations as adequate assessments of core disciplinary knowledge. Another approach draws upon licensure exam scores of recent college graduates in relevant fields, such as education, nursing, and accounting (Miller and Ewell 2005). For instance, the Minnesota Office of Higher Education (2012) reported system-level pass rates on a teacher licensure exam for the University of Minnesota (85 percent), other public universities (97 percent), and private four-year not-for-profit institutions (95 percent). An additional aspirational standard of candidate performance could be established at the 85th percentile, similar to the ETS Recognition of Excellence Award.

Indicator 9: Civic Engagement

A measure of whether college graduates become active citizens provides a final test of educational quality. Civic engagement can be defined as any behaviour that has the intent or effect of influencing matters of public interest, especially the protection, promotion, or provision of public goods and rights (cf. Levine 2007). Zukin et al. (2006) proposed one of the more extensive enumerations of relevant behaviours, including (a) civic indicators (community problem solving, volunteerism, membership in or donations to an association, fundraising); (b) political indicators (voting, persuading others, displaying campaign paraphernalia, donations, volunteering for a campaign); (c) public-voice indicators (contacting officials or media, protesting, signing petitions, boycotting, "buycotting," canvassing); and (d) cognitive engagement (following government affairs and the news, discussing politics, political knowledge). We recommend that states report civic engagement frequencies based on alumni surveys or senior-year surveys, such as NSSE's topical module on civic engagement (NSSE 2017). A central purpose of this type of indicator is to signal to both institutions and stakeholders, especially incoming students, that active citizenship is an expected and highly valued learning outcome.

Utilization of Quality Indicators

The use of quality indicators in accountability systems varies considerably across the United States. An analysis of state and system accountability reports over the past two years revealed twenty states with at least one of the aforementioned indicators of educational quality.[5] This represents a decrease from earlier decades as states dropped quality indicators ostensibly due to the high cost of test administration; loss of political support; changes in leadership; a questionable impact on student learning; and the delegation of student outcomes assessment to regional and program accreditation (Ewell 2009). Most of the states in our analysis used quality indicators for performance reporting, whereas Florida, Kansas, Missouri, Pennsylvania, and Tennessee incorporated indicators within a funding model. For example, Tennessee's "quality assurance funding" model links approximately 5 percent of institutional funding with indicators derived from multiple measures, such as standardized general and major education assessments, program accreditation status, and the NSSE (THEC 2015).

Less clear is the extent to which state efforts to evaluate educational quality have affected institutional practice and student outcomes. On the one hand, state mandates, along with new requirements for regional and program accreditation, have been recognized as a strong impetus for the historical evolution of campus-based student learning assessment (Ewell 2008). In a national survey of provosts from over 600 public postsecondary institutions, respondents rated state and system

5   Interested readers should contact the authors to obtain the related content analysis table.

mandates as a moderate motivational force behind assessment activities, though accreditation was deemed the most important factor (Kuh et al. 2014).[6] Furthermore, on average, provosts indicated that learning assessment results play a moderate role in curricular development, the revision of learning goals, and strategic planning. Respondents assigned less significance to using assessment results for resource allocation and budgeting. On the other hand, rigorous studies of performance funding provide a cautionary note for those who seek to link educational quality measures with state appropriations. Specifically, the preponderance of evidence suggests that performance funding has a negative or null effect on degree productivity, except for potentially small positive effects on the production of short-term certificates (e.g., Hillman, Hicklin Fryar, and Crespín-Trujillo 2017; Rutherford and Rabovsky 2014; Tandberg and Hillman 2014). Among the unintended consequences, institutions exposed to performance funding were more likely to limit the enrolment of racial and ethnic minority students (Umbricht, Fernandez, and Ortagus 2017) and lower-income students (Kelchen and Stedrak 2016).

Despite the expanded institutional capacity for assessment, the impact of quality measurement may be limited on many campuses due to a "compliance culture" that fails to balance the formative and summative functions of evaluation (Ikenberry and Kuh 2015), wherein assessment activities for reporting purposes are decoupled from institutional improvement processes. One innovative way to address this problem is observed in the Multi-State Collaborative to Advance Student Learning (MSC), a national effort involving thirteen states and 900 faculty members at eighty public two- and four-year institutions that aims to improve student learning through direct engagement with faculty and the assessment of authentic student work (Berrett 2016). The MSC eschews the use of standardized exams in favour of a unique assessment approach termed the Valid Assessment of Learning in Undergraduate Education (VALUE). In this approach, faculty evaluators selected from multiple institutions use proficiency criteria specified through VALUE rubrics to rate students' coursework in such areas as critical thinking, writing, and quantitative reasoning. Performance ratings are then shared with both students and their respective instructors, thereby

---

6   The significant role of accreditation is partly due to exhortations in the 1998 federal reauthorization of the Higher Education Act of 1965 for accreditors to emphasize the evaluation of student achievement in reviews of program integrity.

providing faculty with feedback that can be used to improve specific courses. Notably, current reliability and validity limitations may preclude the use of VALUE rubrics for summative purposes (see Carnahan 2016), but the MSC does offer a formative approach to student assessment that might profitably complement present accountability models.

Conclusion

Few issues in higher education deserve the descriptor of crisis more firmly than the problem of quality. Whether one consults research using standardized exams or surveys of employers, a significant proportion of college graduates do not appear to be meeting learning expectations. Furthermore, challenges of inclusive excellence will most certainly become evident at the intersection of quality and equity as lower-income students are channelled to institutions of questionable effectiveness (Mettler 2014) or lack the resources to fully participate in the learning process (e.g., Whatley 2017). Among the first ameliorative steps would be the development of a comprehensive system for assessing the current state of educational practice, institutional effectiveness, and degree integrity with the aim of shaping expectations, providing evidence of student learning, and stimulating improvement. Nothing short of the very possibility of a robust economy and vibrant democracy is at stake.

References

AAC&U (Association of American Colleges and Universities). 2007. *College Learning for the New Global Century: A Report from the National Council for Liberal Education and America's Promise.* Washington, DC: Association of American Colleges and Universities. https://www.aacu.org/sites/default/files/files/LEAP/GlobalCentury_final.pdf

Adelman, Cliff. 2006. *The Toolbox Revisited: Paths to Degree Completion from High School Through College.* Washington, DC: US Department of Education.

Adelman, Cliff, Peter Ewell, Paul Galston, and Carol G. Schneider. 2014. *The Degree Qualifications Profile.* Indianapolis: Lumina Foundation. https://www.luminafoundation.org/files/resources/dqp.pdf

Arum, Richard, and Josipa Roska. 2011. *Academically Adrift: Limited Learning on College Campuses.* Chicago: University of Chicago Press.

Arum, Richard, Josipa Roska, and Amanda Cook. 2016. *Improving Quality in American Higher Education: Learning Outcomes and Assessments for the 21st Century.* San Francisco: Jossey-Bass.

Asmussen, John G., and Aaron S. Horn. 2014. *Developmental Education: A Review of Research on Programmatic Reforms*. Minneapolis: Midwestern Higher Education Compact. http://files.eric.ed.gov/fulltext/ED566747.pdf

Barkley, Elizabeth F. 2009. *Student Engagement Techniques: A Handbook for College Faculty*. San Francisco: Jossey-Bass.

Barrows, Howard S. 1996. "Problem-based Learning in Medicine and Beyond: A Brief Overview." *New Directions for Teaching and Learning* (68): 3–12.

Berrett, Dan. 2016. "The Next Great Hope for Measuring Learning." *The Chronicle of Higher Education*, 16 October. http://www.chronicle.com/article/The-Next-Great-Hope-for/238075

Biggs, John, and Catherine Tang. 2011. *Teaching for Quality Learning at University: What the Student Does*, 4th ed. Berkshire: Open University Press and McGraw-Hill.

Bowman, Nicholas A. 2010. "Can 1st-year College Students Accurately Report Their Learning and Development?" *American Educational Research Journal* 47 (2): 466–96.

———. 2011. "Validity of College Self-reported Gains at Diverse Institutions." *Educational Researcher* 40 (1): 22–4.

Bray, Gayle Babbitt, Ernest T. Pascarella, and Christopher T. Pierson. 2004. "Postsecondary Education and Some Dimensions of Literacy Development: An Exploration of Longitudinal Evidence." *Reading Research Quarterly* 39 (3): 306–30.

Campbell, Corbin M. 2015. "Serving a Different Master: Assessing College Educational Quality for the Public." In *Higher Education: Handbook of Theory and Research* Vol. 30, 525–79. Springer International Publishing.

Campbell, Corbin M., and Alberto F. Cabrera. 2014. "Making the Mark: Are Grades and Deep Learning Related?" *Research in Higher Education* 55 (5): 494–507.

Carnahan, Julie. 2016. *Multi-State Collaborative to Advance Quality Student Learning—Institutes of Education Sciences Grant Application*. Boulder: State Higher Education Executive Officers.

Celio, Christine I., Joseph Durlak, and Allison Dymnicki. 2011. "A Meta-analysis of the Impact of Service-learning on Students." *Journal of Experiential Education* 34 (2): 164–81.

Desjardins, Richard, William Thorn, Andreas Schleicher, Glenda Quintini, Michele Pellizzari, Viktoria Kis, and Ji Eun Chung. 2013. *OECD Skills Outlook 2013: First Results from the Survey of Adult Skills*.

Paris: OECD Publishing. https://www.oecd.org/skills/piaac/Skills%20
volume%201%20(eng)--full%20v12--eBook%20(04%2011%202013).pdf

Dochy, Filip, Mien Segers, Piet Van den Bossche, and David Gijbels.
2003. "Effects of Problem-based Learning: A Meta-analysis." *Learning
and Instruction* 13 (5): 533–68.

Donhardt, Gary L. 2004. "In Search of the Effects of Academic Achievement in Postgraduation Earnings." *Research in Higher Education* 45
(3), 271–84.

Duckworth, Angela L., Patrick D. Quinn, Donald R. Lynam, Rolf Loe-
ber, and Magda Stouthamer-Loeber. 2011. "Role of Test Motivation
in Intelligence Testing." *Proceedings of the National Academy of Sciences*
108 (19): 7716–20.

Eagan, Kevin, Ellen B. Stolzenberg, Jennifer B. Lozano, Melissa C. Ara-
gon, Maria R. Suchard, and Sylvia Hurtado. 2014. *Undergraduate
Teaching Faculty: The 2013–2014 HERI Faculty Survey*. Los Angeles:
Higher Education Research Institute, UCLA. https://pdfs.semantic-
scholar.org/dede/d6df13d5834cab7df13701affe339a1af8a3.pdf

Ewell, Peter T. 2008. "Assessment and Accountability in America Today: Background and Context." *New Directions for Institutional Research*, 2008 (S1): 7–17.

———. 2009. *Assessment, Accountability and Improvement: Revisiting the
Tension*. Champaign, IL: National Institute for Learning Outcomes
Assessment. http://www.learningoutcomeassessment.org/documents/Peter
Ewell_005.pdf

Ewell, Peter T., and Dennis P. Jones. 1996. *Indicators of "Good Practice"
in Undergraduate Education: A Handbook for Development and Implementation*. Boulder, CO: National Center for Higher Education Management. http://files.eric.ed.gov/fulltext/ED403828.pdf

Finney, Sara J., Donna L. Sundre, Matthew S. Swain, and Laura M. Wil-
liams. 2016. "The Validity of Value-added Estimates from Low-stakes
Testing Contexts: The Impact of Change in Test-taking Motivation
and Test Consequences." *Educational Assessment* 21 (1): 60–87.

Francis, Perry C., and Aaron Horn. 2017. "Mental Health Issues and
Counseling Services in US Higher Education: An Overview of Recent
Research and Recommended Practices." *Higher Education Policy* 30
(2): 263–77.

Gonyea, Robert M., and Angie Miller. 2011. "Clearing the AIR about the
Use of Self-reported Gains in Institutional Research." *New Directions
for Institutional Research* 2011 (150): 99–111.

Gordon, Jonathan, Joe Ludlum, and Joseph J. Hoey. 2008. "Validating

NSSE against Student Outcomes: Are They Related?" *Research in Higher Education,* 49 (1): 19–39.

Hart Research Associates. 2015. *Falling Short? College Learning and Career Success.* Washington, DC: Association of American Colleges and Universities. https://www.aacu.org/sites/default/files/files/LEAP/2015employerstudentsurvey.pdf

Harvey, Lee, and Diana Green. 1993. "Defining Quality." *Assessment & Evaluation in Higher Education* 18 (1): 9–34.

Hillman, Nicholas W., Alisa Hicklin Fryar, and Valerie Crespín-Trujillo. 2017. "Evaluating the Impact of Performance Funding in Ohio and Tennessee." *American Educational Research Journal.* doi:0002831217732951

Horn, Aaron S. 2012. "The Cultivation of a Prosocial Value Orientation through Community Service: An Examination of Organizational Context, Social Facilitation, and Duration. *Journal of Youth and Adolescence* 41 (7): 948–68.

Horn, Aaron S. and Gerald W. Fry. 2013. "Promoting Global Citizenship Through Study Abroad: The Influence of Program Destination, Type, and Duration on the Propensity for Development Volunteerism." *VOLUNTAS* 24 (4), 1159–79.

Horn, Aaron S., Olena G. Horner, and Giljae Lee. 2017. "Measuring the Effectiveness of Two-year Colleges: A Comparison of Raw and Value-added Performance Indicators." *Studies in Higher Education:* 1–19.

Horn, Aaron S., and Giljae Lee. 2016. "The Reliability and Validity of Using Regression Residuals to Measure Institutional Effectiveness in Promoting Degree Completion." *Research in Higher Education* 57 (4): 469–96.

———. 2017. "Evaluating the Accuracy of Productivity Indicators in Performance Funding Models." *Educational Policy.* doi:0895904817719521

Huber, Christopher R., and Nathan R. Kuncel. 2016. "Does College Teach Critical Thinking? A Meta-analysis." *Review of Educational Research* 86 (2): 431–68.

Hyytinen, Heidi, Kari Nissinen, Jani Ursin, Auli Toom, and Sari Lindblom-Ylänne. 2015. "Problematising the Equivalence of the Test Results of Performance-based Critical Thinking Tests for Undergraduate Students." *Studies in Educational Evaluation* 44: 1–8.

Ikenberry, Stanley O., and George D. Kuh. 2015. "From Compliance to Ownership: Why and How Colleges and Universities Assess Student Learning." In *Using Evidence of Student Learning to Improve Higher Education,* edited by George Kuh, Stanley O. Ikenberry, Natasha Jankowski, Timothy Reese Cain, Peter T. Ewell, Pat Hutchings, and

Jillian Kinzie, 1–23. San Francisco: Jossey-Bass.

Inkelas, Karen K., and Matthew Soldner. 2011. "Undergraduate Living-learning Programs and Student Outcomes." In *Higher Education: Handbook of Theory and Research,* edited by John C. Smart and Michael B. Paulsen, 1–55. Springer.

Jankowski, Natasha. 2017. *Unpacking Relationships: Instruction and Student Outcomes.* Washington DC: American Council on Education. http://www.acenet.edu/news-room/Documents/Unpacking-Relationships-Instruction-and-Student-Outcomes.pdf

Johnson, David W., Roger T. Johnson, and Karl A. Smith. 1998. "Cooperative Learning Returns to College; What Evidence Is There That It Works?" *Change* 30 (4): 26–35.

Kelchen, Robert, and Luke J. Stedrak. 2016. "Does Performance-based Funding Affect Colleges' Financial Priorities?" *Journal of Education Finance* 41 (3): 302–21.

Khator, Renu. 2011. "Envisioning America's Global University." *U.S. News and World Report,* 13 September. https://www.usnews.com/education/articles/2011/09/13/envisioning-americas-global-university

Klein, Stephen, Ou L. Liu, and James Sconing. 2009. *Test Validity Study Report.* https://cp-files.s3.amazonaws.com/26/TVSReport_Final.pdf

Kornhauser, Zachary G., Jillian Minahan, Karen L. Siedlecki, and Jeffrey T. Steedle. 2014. *A Strategy for Increasing Student Motivation on Low-stakes Assessments.* Council for Aid to Education. http://cae.org/images/uploads/pdf/A_Strategy_for_Increasing_Student_Motivation.pdf

Kuh, George. D. 2008. *High-impact Educational Practices: What They Are, Who Has Access to Them, and Why They Matter.* Washington, DC: Association of American Colleges and Universities.

Kuh, George. D., Natasha Jankowski, Stanley. O. Ikenberry, and Jillian L. Kinzie. 2014. *Knowing What Students Know and Can Do: The Current State of Student Learning Outcomes Assessment in US Colleges and Universities.* Urbana, IL: University of Illinois and Indiana University, National Institute for Learning Outcomes Assessment (NILOA).

Kuh, George. D., Jillian Kinzie, John H. Schuh, and Elizabeth J. Whitt. (2011). *Student Success in College: Creating Conditions that Matter.* Hoboken, NJ: John Wiley & Sons.

Kutner, Mark, Elizabeth Greenberg, Ying Jin, Bridget Boyle, Yung-chen Hsu, and Eric Dunleavy. 2007. *Literacy in Everyday Life: Results from the 2003 National Assessment of Adult Literacy (NCES 2007-480).* US Department of Education. Washington, DC: National Center for Education Statistics. http://files.eric.ed.gov/fulltext/ED495996.pdf

Kyndt, Eva, Elisabeth Raes, Bart Lismont, Fran Timmers, Eduardo Cascallar, and Filip Dochy. 2013. "A Meta-analysis of the Effects of Face-to-face Cooperative Learning. Do Recent Studies Falsify or Verify Earlier Findings?" *Educational Research Review* 10: 133–49.

Levine, Peter. 2007. *The Future of Democracy: Developing the Next Generation of American Citizens.* Medford: Tufts University Press.

Liu, Ou L., Brent Bridgeman, and Rachel M. Adler. 2012. "Measuring Learning Outcomes in Higher Education: Motivation Matters." *Educational Researcher* 41 (9): 352–62.

Liu, Ou L., Joseph A. Rios, and Victor Borden. 2015. "The Effects of Motivational Instruction on College Students' Performance on Low-stakes Assessment." *Educational Assessment* 20 (2): 79–94.

Loes, Chad N., Mark H. Salisbury and Ernest T. Pascarella. 2015. "Student Perceptions of Effective Instruction and the Development of Critical Thinking: A Replication and Extension." *Higher Education* 69 (5): 823–38.

Lumina Foundation. 2016. *States with Higher Education Attainment Goals.* http://strategylabs.luminafoundation.org/wp-content/uploads/2013/10/State-Attainment-Goals.pdf

Markle, Ross, Meghan Brenneman, Teresa Jackson, Jeremy Burrus, and Steven Robbins. 2013. Synthesizing Frameworks of Higher Education Student Learning Outcomes. *ETS Research Report Series* 2013 (2).

Mayer, Richard E. 2011. *Applying the Science of Learning.* Upper Saddle River, NJ: Pearson.

Mayhew, Matthew. J., Nicholas A. Bowman, Alyssa N. Rockenbach, Tricia A. Seifert, and Gregory C. Wolniak. 2016. *How College Affects Students: 21st Century Evidence that Higher Education Works* Vol. 3. San Francisco: Jossey-Bass.

McDonnell, Simon T., Colin C. Chellman, Cheryl B. Littman, and David B. Crook. 2013. Implementing Value-added Accountability Measures at the City University of New York. https://www.cuny.edu/about/administration/offices/ira/opr/papers/accountability_measures.pdf

McCormick Alexander C., Jillian Kinzie, and Robert M. Gonyea. 2013. "Student Engagement: Bridging Research and Practice to Improve the Quality of Undergraduate Education." In *Higher Education: Handbook of Theory and Research* Vol. 28, edited by M. Paulsen. 47–92. Springer: Dordrecht.

Mettler, S. 2014. *Degrees of Inequality: How the Politics of Higher Education Sabotaged the American Dream.* New York: Basic Books.

Miller, Margaret A., and Peter T. Ewell. 2005. *Measuring Up on Col-*

lege-level Learning. National Center for Public Policy and Higher Education. http://www.highereducation.org/reports/mu_learning/Learning.pdf

Minnesota Office of Higher Education. 2012. *Minnesota Measures: 2012 Report on Higher Education Performance*. http://www.ohe.state.mn.us/pdf/MinnesotaMeasures2012.pdf

National Research Council. 2013. *Education for Life and Work: Developing Transferable Knowledge and Skills in the 21st Century*. National Academies Press.

Nelson Laird, Thomas F., Tricia A. Seifert, Ernest T. Pascarella, Matthew J. Mayhew, and Charles F. Blaich. 2014. "Deeply Affecting First-year Students' Thinking: Deep Approaches to Learning and Three Dimensions of Cognitive Development." *The Journal of Higher Education* 85 (3): 402–32.

NSSE (National Survey of Student Engagement). 2017. *NSSE topical modules*. http://nsse.indiana.edu/html/modules.cfm

O'Neil, Harold F., Jamal Abedi, Judy Miyoshi and Ann Mastergeorge. 2005. "Monetary Incentives for Low-stakes Tests." *Educational Assessment* 10 (3): 185–208.

Pascarella, Ernest. T., Mark H. Salisbury, and Charles Blaich. 2011. "Exposure to Effective Instruction and College Student Persistence: A Multi-institutional Replication and Extension." *Journal of College Student Development* 52 (1): 4–19.

Pike, Gary R. 2013. "NSSE Benchmarks and Institutional Outcomes: A Note on the Importance of Considering the Intended Uses of a Measure in Validity Studies." *Research in Higher Education* 54 (2): 149–70.

Porter, Stephen R. 2013. "Self-reported Learning Gains: A Theory and Test of College Student Survey Response." *Research in Higher Education* 54 (2): 201–26.

Reddy, Peter and Elisabeth Moores. 2012. "Placement Year Academic Benefit Revisited: Effects of Demographics, Prior Achievement and Degree Programme." *Teaching in Higher Education* 17 (2): 153–65.

Reindl, Travis, and R. Reyna. 2011. Complete to Compete: From Information to Action—Revamping Higher Education Accountability Systems. *NGA Center for Best Practices*.

Rios, Joseph A., Ou L. Liu, and Brent Bridgeman. 2014. "Identifying Low-Effort Examinees on Student Learning Outcomes Assessment: A Comparison of Two Approaches." *New Directions for Institutional Research* 2014 (161): 69–82.

Roohr, Katrina C., Huili Liu, and Ou L. Liu. 2016. "Investigating Student Learning Gains in College: A Longitudinal Study." *Studies in*

Higher Education 2016: 1–17.

Rutherford, Amanda, and Thomas Rabovsky. 2014. "Evaluating Impacts of Performance Funding Policies on Student Outcomes in Higher Education." *The ANNALS of the American Academy of Political and Social Science* 655 (1): 185–208.

Schneider, Mark, and Lu Yin. 2011. The High Cost of Low Graduation Rates: How Much Does Dropping Out of College Really Cost? *American Institutes for Research.*

Shanghai Ranking Consultancy. 2016. *Academic Ranking of World Universities.* http://www.shanghairanking.com/#

SHEEO (State Higher Education Executive Officers Association). 2005. Accountability for Better Results: A National Imperative for Higher Education.   http://www.sheeo.org/resources/publications/accountability-better-results

Sitzmann, Traci, Katherine Ely, Kenneth G. Brown, and Kristina N. Bauer. 2010. "Self-assessment of Knowledge: A Cognitive Learning or Affective Measure?" *Academy of Management Learning & Education* 9 (2): 169–91.

Sparks, Erin and Mary Jo Waits. 2011. Degrees for What Jobs? Raising Expectations for Universities and Colleges in a Global Economy. *NGA Center for Best Practices.*

Swerdzewski, Peter. J., J. Christine Harmes, and Sara J. Finney. 2011. "Two Approaches for Identifying Low-motivated Students in a Low-Stakes Assessment Context." *Applied Measurement in Education* 24 (2): 162–88.

Tandberg, David A., and Nicholas W. Hillman. 2014. "State Higher Education Performance Funding: Data, Outcomes, and Policy Implications." *Journal of Education Finance* 39 (3): 222–43.

THEC (Tennessee Higher Education Commission). 2015. *Quality Assurance Funding: 2015–20 Cycle Standards.* https://www.tn.gov/assets/entities/thec/attachments/THEC_2015-20_Quality_Assurance_Funding_Guidebook.pdf

Tinto, Vincent. 2012. *Completing College: Rethinking Institutional Action.* Chicago: University of Chicago Press.

US Department of Education. 2006. *A Test of Leadership: Charting the Future of US Higher Education.* https://www2.ed.gov/about/bdscomm/list/hiedfuture/reports/pre-pub-report.pdf

Umbricht, Mark R., Frank Fernandez, and Justin C. Ortagus. 2017. "An Examination of the (Un) Intended Consequences of Performance Funding in Higher Education." *Educational Policy* 31 (5): 643–73.

Warren, Jami L. 2012. "Does Service Learning Increase Student Learning?: A Meta-analysis." *Michigan Journal of Community Service Learning* 18 (2): 56–61.

Weiss, Michael J., Alexander K. Mayer, Dan Cullinan, Alyssa Ratledge, Colleen Sommo, and John Diamond. 2015. "A Random Assignment Evaluation of Learning Communities at Kingsborough Community College—Seven Years Later." *Journal of Research on Educational Effectiveness* 8 (2): 189–217.

Whatley, Melissa 2017. "Financing Study Abroad: An Exploration of the Influence of Financial Factors on Student Study Abroad Patterns." *Journal of Studies in International Education.* doi:1028315317697798

Wise, Steven L., and Christine E. DeMars. 2005. "Low Examinee Effort in Low-stakes Assessment: Problem and Potential Solutions." *Educational Assessment* 10 (1): 1–17.

Yorio, Patrick L., and Feifei Ye. 2012. "A Meta-analysis on the Effects of Service Learning on the Social, Personal, and Cognitive Outcomes of Learning." *Academy of Management Learning & Education* 11 (1): 9–27.

Zhang, Liang. 2008. "The Way to Wealth and the Way to Leisure: The Impact of College Education on Graduates' Earnings and Hours of Work." *Research in Higher Education* 49 (3): 199–213.

Zilberberg, Anna, Sara J. Finney, Kimbery R. Marsh, and Robin D. Anderson. 2014. "The Role of Students' Attitudes and Test-taking Motivation on the Validity of College Institutional Accountability Tests: A Path Analytic Model." *International Journal of Testing* 14 (4): 360–84.

Zilvinskis, John, Anthony A. Masseria, and Gary R. Pike. 2017. "Student Engagement and Student Learning: Examining the Convergent and Discriminant Validity of the Revised National Survey of Student Engagement." *Research in Higher Education* 2017: 1–24.

Zukin, Cliff, Scott Keeter, Molly Andolina, Krista Jenkins, and Michael X. Delli Carpini. 2006. *A New Engagement? Political Participation, Civic Life, and the Changing American Citizen.* Oxford University Press.

2

Quality as Both State and Process: Implications for Performance-Indicator Systems

Alexander C. McCormick and Jillian Kinzie

Performance-indicator systems in higher education involve a conception of accountability—that is, of being answerable for performance—through measures specified *a priori* that are thought to accurately gauge performance. Two approaches dominate, which we call "soft" and "hard" accountability. Soft accountability relies on transparency—public reporting—to render performance visible to the public. The logic is that institutions will be motivated to perform well to sustain public support, successfully recruit students and staff, and so on. Hard accountability, by contrast, ties rewards and sanctions—almost always in the form of funding—to the selected performance metrics. The ideas that we propose in this chapter apply equally to soft and hard approaches.

The use of performance indicators to achieve accountability in higher education is challenging for at least three reasons. First, institutions of higher education perform a range of functions typically comprising undergraduate and graduate education, research and knowledge production, and providing diffuse benefits to the surrounding community (variously defined). Despite rhetoric to the contrary, these functions are not necessarily complementary—attention and resources devoted to one may come at the expense of the others—so whether and how they are combined in an accountability system matters. Having iden-

Assessing Quality in Postsecondary Education: International Perspectives, edited by Harvey P. Weingarten, Martin Hicks, and Amy Kaufman. Montréal and Kingston: McGill-Queen's University Press, Queen's Policy Studies Series. © 2018 The School of Policy Studies, Queen's University at Kingston. All rights reserved.

tified the relevant facets of institutional mission to be included in an accountability system, the second challenge involves distilling these performances into valid and reliable quantitative measures to serve as performance indicators.

The third challenge relates to the assumption underlying indicator-based accountability systems that more (and better) measurement will yield better performance. While this proposition has intuitive appeal and is widely embraced in public management, the mechanisms by which it is thought to work have not been clearly specified and the evidentiary base to support its effectiveness is sparse indeed (see Dubnick 2005). Higher education is a classic example of an environment characterized by task complexity, which "makes both monitoring and incentivizing more difficult while also making capacity, professional norms, and autonomous motivation more important for performance" (Jakobsen et al. 2017, 2).

Research into the impact of performance funding in higher education has found mixed effects, including some that were unlikely to have been envisioned or intended (Hillman, Fryar, and Crespín-Trujillo, 2018; Tandberg and Hillman 2014). For example, in studying long-standing performance funding regimes in two US states, Hillman, Fryar, and Crespín-Trujillo (2018) found no effect on bachelor's degree production, negative effects on associate's degree production, and positive effects in one state on certificate production—suggesting that in response to perceived incentives, some of that state's community colleges may have emphasized the production of short-term certificates at the expense of associate's degree production. This underscores the imperative to carefully consider the likely behavioural response to an accountability system on the part of affected higher-education institutions.

In addition to considering the design characteristics of an indicator system, it is important to consider the requirements for a good indicator. Here we are guided by the work of the US National Forum on Education Statistics (2005), which identified five essential characteristics of a good indicator: usefulness (i.e., relevance), validity, reliability, timeliness, and cost-effectiveness (the information value justifies the cost of collection). To this list we add "actionability"—to be useful, an indicator must inform decision makers about purposeful and responsible intervention to drive improvement.

Two Dimensions of Educational Quality

For the purposes of this chapter, we assume that the quality of undergraduate education is an essential focus of an accountability system. We argue for a reconceptualization of educational quality to incorporate both static and dynamic elements. The static dimension represents a snapshot of performance at a moment in time—the conventional approach to accountability—while the dynamic dimension recognizes that performance can change over time, and that using results to improve performance is a vital sign of an effective high-performing organization. Incorporating both dimensions in a performance-indicator system offers a promising approach to evaluating institutions' potential to reach or surpass key objectives and we believe it is more likely to affect positive change by leveraging professional norms and autonomous motivation—both powerful forces in the academy that should be leveraged rather than ignored or seen as obstacles to be overcome.

Our proposed two-dimensional performance-indicator system includes traditional and expanded "static" measures of performance, plus "dynamic" measures of evidence use in a quality-improvement process. Traditional measures of performance in higher education, including enrolment, retention rates, degree completion, and student satisfaction, are widely used static indicators of performance, in part because they are readily available or easily collected. However, they bear little relation to student learning and are thus insufficient proxies for educational quality, particularly as it relates to two key goals of higher education: student learning and success. If these measures form the core of a performance-indicator system, they risk the problem of goal displacement in which decision makers focus attention and resources on how to improve those proxy measures without regard to the quality of education delivered (Figure 2.1). Renowned scholar of organizations, James March, concisely expresses the problem of goal displacement: "A system of performance rewards linked to precise measures is not an incentive to perform well; it is an incentive to obtain a good score" (March 1984, 28).

To fully and faithfully assess educational quality, key measures of teaching and learning are needed. Performance indicators must incorporate evidence of teaching and learning, including meaningful measures of the learning process and outcomes. We further argue that the performance system must attend to the use of evidence in service of quality improvement. Attention to both measures of learning process

Figure 2.1

Goal Displacement Resulting from the Use of Proxy Measures

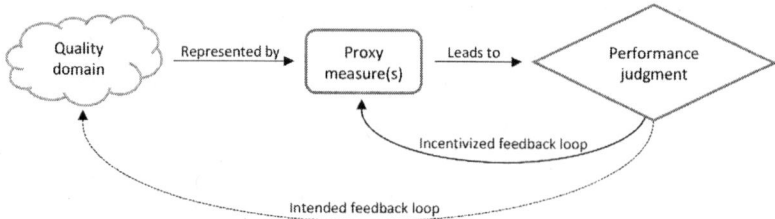

Source: McCormick (2017)

or outcomes, and of evidence-informed improvement would recognize and reward institutions that link knowledge about performance to improvement initiatives.

The Static Dimension

Static measures of teaching and learning focused on educational processes and learning outcomes are necessary elements of performance-indicator systems of educational quality. Metrics that demonstrate the extent to which students experience practices that matter to achievement and success are important indicators of educational quality. Drawing on the work of the US-based National Survey of Student Engagement (NSSE) and the decades of research on which it rests, we recommend measures of academic challenge, collaborative learning, and student-faculty interaction; participation in high-impact practices (HIPs) such as undergraduate research, service-learning, and internships (Kuh 2008); and an emphasis on cognitive tasks associated with deep learning including reflection, integration, and higher-order learning as well as engaging with diverse perspectives (Marton and Säljö 1984). NSSE's Engagement Indicators (EIs) provide valid, reliable, actionable information about distinct aspects of student engagement that matter to educational quality. These measures draw appropriate attention to student learning by focusing on factors that contribute to desired outcomes.

Measures of student engagement, in particular the amount of time and effort students dedicate to coursework, as well as the extent to which students experience collaborative learning and perceive the environment to be supportive of their learning, are positively associated with student learning, institutional persistence, and graduation rates (McCormick, Kinzie, and Gonyea 2013; NSSE 2016). Similarly, measures of deep approaches to learning, reflected in scores on NSSE's Higher-order Learning and Reflective and Integrative Learning EIs, provide important measures of academic challenge that signal an emphasis on critical thinking. Students who experience deep learning tend to earn higher grades, persist at higher rates, integrate and transfer information at higher levels, and also report enjoying learning (Biggs 2003; Ramsden 2003; Tagg 2003; Van Rossum and Schenk 1984).

Other important educational process metrics related to student learning outcomes assess teaching clarity and organized instruction. Blaich et al. (2016) identified aspects of teaching clarity and organization, such as the extent to which faculty interpret ideas and theories clearly, give clear explanations, and clearly explain course goals and requirements, that had a significant impact on student growth on a set of learning outcomes assessed in a rigorous pre/post design. Students who reported higher levels of teaching clarity and organization were more likely to experience gains in critical thinking, socially responsible leadership, interest in diversity, and need for cognition. Experiencing clear and organized instruction was also positively related to the extent to which students engage in higher-order learning, reflective learning, and integrative learning (Wang et al. 2015). These measures—some of which are reflected in NSSE's Effective Teaching Practices EI, as well as in many institutions' end-of-course evaluations, and sometimes as elements of academic program assessment—also merit consideration as educational process performance metrics.

A final example of an educational process measure associated with positive student outcomes involves participation in HIPs, including educationally enriching experiences such as learning communities, undergraduate research, service-learning, internships and field placements, and writing-intensive courses (Kuh 2008; Kuh and O'Donnell 2013). Many institutions already use measures of HIP participation in their strategic indicators and performance dashboards. For example, the University of Massachusetts Lowell created a report card to track the proportion of students in HIPs, including baseline indicators and goals for 2018 (NSSE 2015). In their study of college and university performance dashboards, Terkla et al. (2012) found that nearly 70 percent of the dashboards included measures of student participation in study abroad, undergraduate research, and service learning along with other measures of the student experience. Tracking participation in enriching educational experiences such as these focuses attention on learning opportunities that students often describe as transformative and life-changing.

An important consideration for the inclusion of educational process measures in performance indicators is data quality. Expanded measures of educational process should satisfy standard data quality criteria of reliability and validity. However, it is also critical that the measures are relevant to institutions, are actionable, and that they emphasize aspects of consequential validity—that is, they must have utility for institutional improvement. Because measures should be useful to institutions in their efforts to improve undergraduate education, an important criterion to consider is whether they are "fit for purpose" (Harvey and Green 1993). In this context, fitness for purpose depends on how the metric or information will be used, and implies that metrics provide meaningful input to quality improvement initiatives developed by the institution.

NSSE's practical aim is to provide participating institutions with diagnostic information about the student experience that can be influenced in practice and that an array of educators and institutional leaders can address. The core goal of the project is to facilitate the use of survey results to inform the improvement of undergraduate education. While the concept of student engagement is very much about what students do, responsibility for promoting engagement rests with the institution (McCormick, Kinzie, and Gonyea 2013). NSSE's role in stimulating and informing institutional improvement efforts has been demonstrated in the more than 500 accounts of NSSE data use (Kinzie, Cogswell, and Wheatle 2015; NSSE 2017), and has led to the development of approaches to data use and theorizing about the scholarship of practice (Kinzie 2017; Kinzie and Pennipede 2009).

Performance indicators must be useful to guide improvements in teaching and learning. To evaluate the metrics against their purpose as a tool for improvement, we can look to a concept suggested in higher-education assessment. This concept is the expectation that assessment results, in this case performance indicators, are "good enough" to use. The "good enough" criterion suggests that the quality of evidence is less about precise measures based on methodological perfection, and more about measures that are practically useful (Upcraft and Schuh 2002). Blaich and Wise (2011) emphasized the good-enough criterion in relation to motivating action on evidence. They suggest that assessment studies be evaluated for the extent to which they allow educators to consider the evidence good enough "to try something different that might benefit our students" (Blaich and Wise 2011, 13). The emphasis on a good-enough criterion for performance metrics underscores the importance of actionability; that measures be useful for improvement.

The Dynamic Dimension

While performance-indicator systems in higher education typically reflect a desire for greater accountability, the true purpose of performance indicators should be to bring about improvement (Gaither 1997; Gaither, Nedwek, and Neal 1994). The goal of improvement is thus the focus of the second dimension of our proposed performance-indicator system for educational quality. This represents the dynamic side of the system, focusing on the use of evidence for improvement. It thus reflects the extent to which the static measures help institutions understand whether they are on the right track for success—and if not, where to focus attention. The dynamic dimension explicitly links the performance system to educational improvement.

The dynamic dimension of our performance-indicator system emerges from the growth of large-scale assessment in institutions of higher education. Assessment, or the systematic collection, review, and use of information for the purpose of improvement, has come to encompass a broad process of evaluating institutional performance and effectiveness (Banta and Palomba 2015). Over the last decade, universities have greatly increased their levels of assessment activity and, in particular, their collection of a variety of forms of evidence of educational effectiveness and measures of student learning (Kuh et al. 2015). The use of data in the course of institutional decision making has also emerged as a key strategy to foster improvement (Coburn and Turner 2012). Correspondingly, institutions report using evidence at higher levels to improve undergraduate education (Kuh et al. 2015). It is clear that colleges and universities have more forms of assessment information and some seem to be using this evidence in improvement processes. However, the use at most institutions is primarily for compliance reporting and represents a nascent level of transparency and evidence use.

We know little about the actual practice of data use. According to Coburn and Turner (2012), most of the writing about data use in higher education is normative, championing the cause of data use for improvement. The small body of extant research focuses on describing either activities involved in data use or the outcomes of data use. This work offers little insight into what mechanisms produce the outcomes and provides little to no information about how individuals interact with data and how this contributes to various outcomes.

More research on the practice of data use in higher education is clearly needed. However, institutional assessment activities have clearly matured to the state of having ample information about institutional effectiveness and even established structures for using evidence to guide improvement. This level of assessment practice suggests the potential for representing effectiveness of data use as a vital component of a performance-indicator system that seeks to promote educational improvement.

Development of Dynamic Indicators

To consider the dynamic dimension of educational quality, we draw on literature and practical projects related to the use of evidence to guide improvement. Specifically, we discuss the US-based National Institute for Learning Outcomes Assessment's (NILOA) Transparency Framework and the related Excellence in Assessment (EIA) award established in 2016. We also consider and adapt a developmental rubric for the use of assessment created by the Higher Learning Commission (HLC) of the North Central Association of Colleges and Schools, an accrediting body in the US.

To model how colleges and universities should use data and represent it for internal and external audiences, NILOA developed the Transparency Framework (NILOA 2011). The framework distinguishes six aspects of transparency of institutional websites with regard to providing evidence of student learning, including the explicit specification of learning outcomes; plans for gathering evidence; training provided to faculty and staff to help them understand, develop, implement, communicate, and use evidence; information on assessment activities underway; results from assessment; and the use of evidence. This final component, the use of evidence, which represents the extent to which evidence of student learning informs problem identification, decision making, planning, goal setting, faculty development, program review, course revision, and other accountability and performance improvement initiatives, is most relevant to our discussion. The transparent use of evidence involves the communication of evidence to particular audiences including faculty, staff, administrators, students, and governing boards, to facilitate the use of assessment results to identify areas where changes in policies and practices can lead to improvement.

After several years of promoting the framework and documenting exemplary institutional practices, NILOA and three higher-education organizations partnered to create the Excellence in Assessment (EIA) designation to recognize institutions for their efforts in intentional integration of campus-level learning-outcomes assessment (Kinzie et al. 2017). The EIA assessment is based on eight categories of criteria, one of which relates explicitly to the use of student learning evidence and offers standards for exemplary practice in using data for improvement. These criteria define exemplary use of student learning evidence in four areas: integrating institution-level results with evidence gathered at other levels, sharing the use of evidence with stakeholders, communicating changes made as a result of evidence, and monitoring and communicating the results of these changes (Table 2.1). These four areas in the EIA rubric define exemplary practice and suggest possible performance metrics related to data use.

HLC created a rubric for assessment use indicating an institution's level of development on the assessment implementation continuum (Lopez 2002). The model features three levels—beginning, making progress, and maturing—each with indicative characteristics. This matrix suggests the potential for a similar developmental approach to evidence-informed improvement in the dynamic side of a performance-indicator system. Adapted from the HLC model, Table 2.2 depicts three levels of development with regard to evidence-informed improvement—underdeveloped, progressing, and mature—each with associated characteristics or attributes.

Signals and Artifacts of Evidence Use

The aforementioned frameworks can inform the development of dynamic measures of evidence-informed improvement. This approach complements static indicators by documenting how evidence is considered and used, and modeling mature processes for evidence use. Whereas the static dimension is well established with associated measurement approaches, higher education is in the early stages of specifying indicators of evidence use to guide improvement. In addition, a wide range of performative acts by an institution can signify evidence use. Reducing the dynamic dimension to a fixed set of counts or ratios risks excessive simplification and standardization as well as vulnerability to the goal

… continued on page 38

Table 2.1

Excellence in Assessment Criteria Related to Evidence Use

Criterion	Standard of Excellence
Integration of campus-level results with measures used at other levels to guide campus decision making	Campus-level assessment results have been considered in combination with assessment results at other levels of the institution to guide decision making related to changes in policies and practices that may lead to improved student learning.
Evidence of use of assessment results from all levels of campus provided to stakeholders	Stakeholders from both inside and outside the institution are regularly provided with evidence that institutional decision making is appropriately guided by assessment results from multiple levels of campus assessment.
Communication of changes made as a result of assessment evidence from all levels of campus	Changes made as a result of assessment results are communicated both to internal and external campus audiences, including students. Communications include information on evidence supporting the need for change.
Communication of outcomes from changes made as a result of assessment evidence from all levels of campus	Changes made as a result of assessment results are monitored and evaluated. Outcomes from changes are communicated both to internal and external campus audiences, including students. Communications include information on evidence used to evaluate the change.

Source: Excerpted and adapted from NILOA (2017).

Table 2.2

Developmental Stages of Evidence-informed Improvement and Associated Characteristics

Stage	Characteristics
Underdeveloped	Limited evidence of evidence-informed improvement activity, or developing slowly, or stalled
	• Sufficient collection of evidence, but few established structures or processes for examining and acting on data
	• Performance metrics may be set and monitored, but they are not widely shared, and there are no expectations for reporting plans for improvement informed by these metrics
	• Limited assessment of the results of improvement initiatives
Progressing	Demonstrated use of evidence to improve student learning experiences; comparing performance against specified goals
	• Performance metrics and reports are shared, and include interpretation of results and action plans
	• Results reference standards, comparable measures, and what it will take to reach stated goals
	• Some examples of evidence-informed decision making
	• Some sharing of changes made as a result of evidence
	• Some efforts to assess the results of improvement initiatives
Mature	Structured, systematic, ongoing evidence-informed action; routine monitoring of the impact of changes made; results disaggregated to observe impact on particular student populations
	• Evidence-informed action is standard; processes are public and structured to incorporate data, and to reveal the use of data in decisions
	• Performance metrics are public, shared, and include attention to processes for interpreting and using data, how data influences action, and what action is underway
	• Changes made in response to evidence are widely communicated
	• Implications of performance evidence for improving educational practice and policies are clearly identified and communicated
	• Metrics are rigorously monitored, disaggregated by student populations, and used to evaluate the outcome of improvement initiatives

Source: Adapted from Lopez (2002).

displacement problem discussed earlier. Given these concerns, we adopt the language of signals and artifacts rather than specific metrics, but our intent is, nonetheless, to set high expectations for what signifies serious, committed, and sustained use of evidence to inform improvement. Mere rhetorical statements are not sufficient: signals and artifacts must reflect verifiable actions related to the use of evidence for improvement.

We propose four categories of signals and artifacts: communicating evidence, evidence-informed action plans, implementation, and loop closing. We elaborate on this model below, with examples of indicative signals and artifacts.

Communicating Evidence. Communicating evidence means more than merely reporting on evidence gathering. The communication must include specific results and interpretation with a discussion of implications for the institution, and also regular opportunities for internal and external audiences to collectively make meaning of results. What demonstrates that an institution shares assessment results and their meaning with important internal and external stakeholders? Indicative signals and artifacts include:

- Results circulated to internal leadership (deans, department chairs, relevant committees, student government, governing board, etc.), faculty, and staff in the form of reports, strategic plans, websites, and other displays
- Results circulated to external constituents (governmental bodies, alumni, news media, etc.) in the form of websites, annual reports, and other displays
- Use of common reporting templates across all programs and units that require elaboration of the process and frequency of data collection, discussion of results, and interpretation of evidence
- Systematic and documented occasions for internal and external constituents to collectively interpret evidence

Evidence-informed Action Plans. The emphasis here is on the development of concrete plans linked to the needs identified by evidence, including verifiable organizational behaviours intended to put those plans into effect and assess their impact. What demonstrates that examination and communication of assessment results and their meaning leads to concrete plans to address the concerns and shortcomings revealed by the evidence? Indicative signals and artifacts include:

- Reports that connect evidence to the logical next steps to address needs identified in the communication of evidence, including discussion of possible action plans and rationale for choosing among them

- Assessment plans that call on programs and units to report what actions will be taken in response to identified needs
- Formation of committees and other groups charged with the development of actions plans in response to identified needs
- Allocation of institutional resources to support implementation of action plans
- Explicit identification of organizational units (e.g., offices, departments, programs) responsible for implementation, shared with internal and/or external stakeholders
- Dissemination of timelines, milestones, and intended outcomes for implementation shared with internal and/or external stakeholders
- *A priori* design of how action plans will be evaluated (what will success look like)

Implementation. Implementation is where the rubber hits the road: Well-designed and sincere evidence-informed action plans have no value until they are put into effect. Verifiable implementation signals the difference between blue-sky thinking and the hard work of organizational change. What demonstrates the transition from planning to action? Indicative signals and artifacts include:

- Prototyping or pilot testing proposed plans with feedback mechanisms to inform the final design
- Commissioning of internal or external evaluators
- Dissemination of new programs and activities to internal and/or external stakeholders
- Full documentation of the process for using evidence to guide implementation
- Documentation of administrative or academic changes, such as modifications to technology, training, curriculum, policies, or organizational structure made in response to assessment evidence

Loop closing. Loop closing refers to monitoring and evaluation processes to assess the impact of implemented plans. Did the plans achieve their purposes? Were there unintended consequences? Indicative signals and artifacts include:

- Feedback processes involving those most directly responsible for implementation as well as those most affected (e.g., students)

- Evidence-gathering to inform the evaluation plan created during the implementation phase
- Progress reports issued by organizational units responsible for implementation of action plans at key milestones, shared with relevant internal and/or external stakeholders
- Adjustments and course corrections made during the implementation phase
- Development and use of rubrics specifying elements and levels of goal achievement (e.g., missing, developing, satisfactory, and exemplary), such as connecting results and program changes, learning-outcome changes, assessment-method changes, and evaluating the extent to which a unit has closed the loop
- Reports that identify successes and lessons learned as well as recommendations for adjustments or new action plans, shared with relevant internal and/or external stakeholders
- Narrative of how assessment results have been used to showcase or promote student learning success or program achievements in student learning, and how this has been communicated to specific target audiences

To be sure, the signals and artifacts listed above represent proxy measures of evidence-informed improvement, but our approach has been to identify indicators that correspond closely to the stages and activities of evidence use. Indeed, they constitute a simplified playbook for using evidence to guide improvement initiatives.

Future Directions

The development of a dynamic measure of evidence-informed improvement representing four categories of signals and artifacts necessitates a focus on verifiable actions. The categories and indicators also communicate expectations for the practice of using evidence for improvement. The categories could be further developed as dimensions of a rubric with criteria that define stages of evidence use such as initial, emerging, developed, and highly developed.

Although the indicative signals and artifacts proposed above aim to render conceptions of evidence use concrete, the model may not recognize the full range of evidence use to improve institutional performance. Arguing that most conceptions of data use for improvement overlook efforts that meaningfully lead to improvement, Jonson, Guetterman, and Thompson (2014) proposed an innovative model of evidence use adapted from the literature on evaluation. They argue that a range of meanings are attached to the term "use of evidence," noting, like Weiss (1979), that such use occurs through a complex process by which decision makers access evidence, use experience, are influenced by pressure, and make judgments in interconnected ways to inform themselves and make decisions. More to the point, "use" represents more than a direct, observable action for change. Rather, use of evidence for improvement may be better construed as "influence."

Two aspects of influence in Jonson, Guetterman, and Thompson's (2014) schema are relevant to next-generation discussions of the dynamic dimension of educational quality. The first is the "effects of influence," or the processes and functions that link static performance measures to educational practices, policies, and outcomes. The authors identify four distinct subtypes of effects including "instrumental," which refers to an influence that prompts a direct action akin to the model that we have proposed above; "conceptual" includes an influence on understanding or ways of thinking; "affect" references an influence on attitudes or emotions; and "affirmation," which refers to an influence that supports an existing policy or practice.

The second relevant aspect of influence—"results of use"—references more typical understandings about the use of evidence including improved outcomes, but it also incorporates personal transformation, building communities of practice, and generating symbolic or political support. This second aspect is useful for understanding the organizational effects of performance metrics and their impact on educational effectiveness and improvement. The reconceptualization of the influence of evidence to include more affective dimensions such as the extent to which beliefs and attitudes are shaped, persons and practices are transformed, and communities of practice are built, offers an enriched model for understanding how organizations learn from evidence.

Conclusion

A comprehensive system of indicators for evaluating the quality of undergraduate education should consider two dimensions of quality: the static dimension, which examines performance at a moment in time, and the dynamic dimension, which takes into account the imperative for higher-education institutions to use performance information to guide improvement initiatives. While the static dimension is common to performance-indicator systems, incorporating the improvement-oriented dynamic dimension would represent a major innovation. Based on the literature on accountability, as well as studies of performance funding in the United States, we believe the focus on improvement will help address the limitations of performance-indicator systems based on proxy measures of performance. We further believe that a focus on evidence-informed improvement leverages the unique characteristics and power dynamics that characterize the modern university, specifically given the powerful role of academic norms and autonomy on the part of those most responsible for educational quality: academic leaders and instructional staff. Finally, incorporating explicit incentives for demonstrating evidence-informed improvement activity calls attention to the development of relevant capacities and practices.

We argue for a set of static measures that focus attention on activities, behaviours, and experiences that are empirically linked to desired learning outcomes. Examples include measures of academic challenge, collaborative learning, and student-faculty interaction; participation in high-impact practices, such as undergraduate research, service-learning, and internships; and cognitive tasks associated with deep learning including reflection, integration, and higher-order learning as well as engaging with diverse perspectives. These measures satisfy the criteria for good indicators established by the National Forum on Education Statistics (2005): They are useful, valid, reliable, timely, and cost-effective, and they have the added (and we argue, crucial) benefit of being actionable. Given the innovative nature of our call for dynamic measures of evidence-informed improvement, we recommend a focus on what we call signals and artifacts—verifiable products of a range of performative acts that signify a genuine commitment to evidence-informed improvement. We propose four categories of actions that signify evidence-informed improvement: communicating evidence, action plans, implementation, and loop closing.

Missing from this discussion is a consideration of the actors responsible for designing and implementing such a system. There is a strong argument to be made for a highly collaborative approach involving policy makers as well as personnel from the university system and individual institutions in crafting a system that will motivate the right behaviours. This calls to mind Richard Elmore's important piece on "backward mapping" that called for a profound shift in how we conceptualize the problem of policy implementation. Elmore (1980) notes that forward mapping—that is, a top-down approach in which policy makers specify the goals to be achieved by agents responsible for implementing policy, and the specific arrangements and configurations required for implementation—rests on the questionable assumption that "policymakers control the organizational, political, and technological processes that affect implementation" (Elmore 1980, 603). Elmore calls instead to start at the ground level of policy implementation and then work backwards to determine at each level what is most likely to produce the desired outcomes:

> The logic of backward mapping…begins not at the top of the implementation process but at the last possible stage, the point at which administrative actions intersect private choices. It begins not with a statement of intent, but with a statement of the specific behavior at the lowest level of the implementation process that generates the need for a policy. Only after that behavior is described does the analysis presume to state an objective; the objective is first stated as a set of organizational operations and then as a set of effects, or outcomes, that will result from these operations. Having established a relatively precise target at the lowest level of the system, the analysis backs up through the structure of implementing agencies, asking at each level two questions: What is the ability of this unit to affect the behavior that is the target of the policy? And what resources does this unit require in order to have that effect? In the final stage of analysis the analyst or policymaker describes a policy that directs resources at the organizational units likely to have the greatest effect (Elmore 1980, 604).

The relevance of the argument to any system intended to improve performance in higher education is inescapable and justifies approaching system design in close collaboration with those whose actions will determine success. Similarly, the need for collaboration extends to the organizational behaviours for using evidence. Expectations for evidence use necessitate a commitment to broadly sharing results with faculty, staff, and others whose collaboration in the interpretation of evidence, development and implementation of action plans, and impact assessment is vital to achieving improvement on the ground.

Although we urge a reconceptualization of educational quality, one comprising static and dynamic dimensions that are each amenable to measurement, we must also temper the enthusiasm for performance measurement with the words of accountability scholars Melvin Dubnick and George Frederickson: "Performance measures are best understood as information that may help sharpen questions rather than the answers to questions. Such measures, particularly in fields with elusive bottom lines, are best thought of as clues, interpretations, impressions, and useful input rather than facts. And of course all such interpretations carry with them certain biases, assumptions, and values" (Dubnick and Frederickson 2011, 32).

References

Banta, Trudy W., and Catherine A. Palomba. 2015. *Assessment Essentials: Planning, Implementing, and Improving Assessment in Higher Education,* 2nd ed. San Francisco: Jossey-Bass.

Biggs, John B. 2003. *Teaching for Quality Learning at University: What the Student Does,* 2nd ed. Buckingham: Open University Press.

Blaich, Charles, and Kathleen Wise. 2011. *From Gathering to Using Assessment Results: Lessons from the Wabash National Study.* Occasional Paper No. 8. Champaign, IL: National Institute for Learning Outcomes Assessment.

Blaich, Charles, Kathleen Wise, Ernest T. Pascarella, and Josipa Roksa. 2016. "Instructional Clarity and Organization: It's Not New or Fancy, But It Matters." *Change* 48 (4): 6–13.

Coburn, Cynthia E., and Erica O. Turner. 2012. "The Practice of Data Use: An Introduction." *American Journal of Education* 118 (2): 99–111.

Dubnick, Melvin. 2005. "Accountability and the Promise of Performance: In Search of the Mechanisms." *Public Performance & Management Review* 28 (3): 376–417.

Dubnick, Melvin, and George H. Frederickson. 2011. *Public Accountability: Performance Measurement, the Extended State, and the Search for Trust.* National Academic of Public Administration and The Kettering Foundation.

Elmore, Richard F. 1980. "Backward Mapping: Implementation Research and Policy Decisions." *Political Science Quarterly* 94 (4): 601–16.

Gaither, Gerald. 1997. "Performance-indicator systems as Instruments for Accountability and Assessment." *Assessment Update* 9 (1): 1.

Gaither, Gerald, Brian Nedwek, and John Neal. 1994. *Measuring Up: The Promises and Pitfalls of Performance Indicators in Higher Education. ASHE-ERIC Higher Education Report,* No. 5. Washington: Association for the Study of Higher Education; ERIC Clearinghouse on Higher Education.

Harvey, Lee, and Diana Green. 1993. "Defining Quality." *Assessment and Evaluation in Higher Education* 18 (1) 9–34.

Hillman, Nicholas W., Alisa Hicklin Fryar, and Valerie Crespín-Trujillo. 2018. "Evaluating the Impact of Performance Funding in Ohio and Tennessee." *American Educational Research Journal* 55 (1): 144–70.

Jakobsen, Mads L., Martin Baekgaard, Donald P. Moynihan, and Nina van Loon. 2017. "Making Sense of Performance Regimes: Rebalancing External Accountability and Internal Learning." *Perspectives on Public Management and Governance.* https://doi.org/10.1093/ppmgov/gvx001

Jonson, Jessica L., Tim Guetterman, and Robert J. Thompson Jr. 2014. "An Integrated Model of Influence: Use of Assessment Data in Higher Education." *Research and Practice in Assessment* 9: 18–30.

Kinzie, Jillian. 2017. "The Use of Student Engagement Findings as a Case of Evidence-based Practice." In *Toward a Scholarship of Practice. New Directions for Higher Education*, edited by John Braxton, 47–56. San Francisco: Jossey-Bass.

Kinzie, Jillian, Cynthia A. Cogswell, and Katherine I. E. Wheatle. 2015. "Reflections on the State of Student Engagement Data Use and Strategies for Action." *Assessment Update* 27 (2): 1–2, 14–16.

Kinzie, Jillian, Teri L. Hinds, Natasha A. Jankowski, and Terrel L. Rhodes. 2017. "Recognizing Excellence in Assessment." *Assessment Update* 29 (1): 1–2, 15–16.

Kinzie, Jillian, and Barbara S. Pennipede. 2009. "Converting Engagement Results into Action." In *Using NSSE in Institutional Research. New Directions for Institutional Research*, No. 141, edited by Robert M. Gonyea and George D. Kuh, 83–106. San Francisco: Jossey Bass.

Kuh, George D. 2008. *High-impact Educational Practices: What They Are, Who Has Access to Them, and Why They Matter.* Washington, DC: Association of American Colleges and Universities.

Kuh, George D., Stanley O. Ikenberry, Natasha A. Jankowski, Timothy R. Cain, Peter E. Ewell, Pat Hutchings, and Jillian Kinzie. 2015. *Using Evidence of Student Learning to Improve Higher Education.* San Francisco: Jossey-Bass.

Kuh, George D., and Ken O'Donnell. 2013. *Ensuring Quality & Taking High-impact Practices to Scale.* Washington, DC: Association of American Colleges and Universities.

Lopez, Cecilia. 2002. "Assessment of Student Learning: Challenges and Strategies." *Journal of Academic Librarianship* 28 (6): 356–67.

March, James G. 1984. "How We Talk and How We Act: Administrative Theory and Administrative Life." In *Leadership and Organizational Culture: New Perspectives on Administrative Theory and Practice*, edited by Thomas J. Sergiovanni and John E. Corbally, 18–35. Champaign, IL: University of Illinois Press.

Marton, Ference, and Roger Säljö. 1984. "Approaches to Learning." In *The Experience of Learning*, edited by Ference Marton, Dani J. Hounsell, and Noel J. Entwistle, 39–58. Edinburgh: Scottish Academic.

McCormick, Alexander C. 2017. "The Intersection of Rankings with University Quality, Public Accountability, and Institutional Improvement." In *Global Rankings and the Geopolitics of Higher Education: Understanding the Influence and Impact of Rankings on Higher Education, Policy and Society*, edited by Ellen Hazelkorn, 205–215. London: Routledge.

McCormick, Alexander C., Jillian Kinzie, and Robert M. Gonyea. 2013. "Student Engagement: Bridging Research and Practice to Improve the Quality of Undergraduate Education." In *Higher Education: Handbook of Theory and Research, Vol. 28*, edited by Michael B. Paulsen, 47–92. Dordrecht: Springer.

National Forum on Education Statistics. 2005. *Forum Guide to Education Indicators*. Washington, DC: National Center for Education Statistics. https://nces.ed.gov/pubs2005/2005802.pdf

NILOA (National Institute for Learning Outcomes Assessment). 2011. *Transparency Framework*. Urbana, IL: University of Illinois and Indiana University, National Institute for Learning Outcomes Assessment. http://www.learningoutcomeassessment.org/TransparencyFrameworkIntro.htm

———. 2017. *Excellence in Assessment Designation Evaluation Rubric*. http://www.learningoutcomesassessment.org/eiadesignation.html

NSSE (National Survey of Student Engagement). 2015. *Lessons from the Field–Volume 3: Using Data to Catalyze Change on Campus*. Bloomington, IN: Center for Postsecondary Research, Indiana University School of Education. http://nsse.indiana.edu/pdf/LFF_3.pdf

———. 2016. *Engagement Insights: Survey Findings on the Quality of Undergraduate Education—Annual Results 2016*. Bloomington, IN: Center for Postsecondary Research, Indiana University School of Education. http://nsse.indiana.edu/html/annual_results.cfm

———. 2017. *Lessons from the Field–Volume 4: Digging Deeper to Focus and Extend Data Use*. Bloomington, IN: Center for Postsecondary Research, Indiana University School of Education. http://nsse.indiana.edu/pdf/LFF_4.pdf

Ramsden, Paul. 2003. *Learning to Teach in Higher Education*. London: Routledge.

Tagg, John. 2003. *The Learning Paradigm College*. Boston: Anker.

Tandberg, David A., and Nicholas W. Hillman. 2014. "State Higher Education Performance Funding: Data, Outcomes, and Policy Implications. *Journal of Education Finance* 39 (2): 222–43.

Terkla, Dawn G., Jessica Sharkness, Margaret Cohen, Heather S. Roscoe, and Marjorie Wiseman. 2012. *Institutional Dashboards: Navigational Tool for Colleges and Universities. AIR Professional File, No. 123*. Tallahassee: Association for Institutional Research. https://www.airweb.org/EducationAndEvents/Publications/Documents/123.pdf

Upcraft, M. Lee, and John Schuh. 2002. "Assessment vs. Research: Why We Should Care about the Difference." *About Campus* 7 (1): 16–20.

Van Rossum, E. J., and Simone M. Schenk. 1984. "The Relationship Between Learning Conception, Study Strategy and Learning Outcome." *British Journal of Educational Psychology* 54 (1): 73–83.

Wang, Jui-Sheng, Ernest T. Pascarella, Thomas F. Nelson Laird, and Amy K. Ribera. 2015. "How Clear and Organized Classroom Instruction and Deep Approaches to Learning Affect Growth in Critical Thinking and Need for Cognition." *Studies in Higher Education*, 40 (10): 1786–807.

Weiss, Carol. 1979. "The Many Meanings of Research Utilization." *Public Administration Review* 39 (5): 426–31.

3

The Role of Generic Skills in Measuring Academic Quality

Roger Benjamin

Introduction

The goal of this chapter is to demonstrate why measuring student learning outcomes in undergraduate education is essential to understanding the concept of academic quality, including its critical role in measuring and improving academic quality. This aim is supported by addressing five topics: (1) the link between the generic-skills concept and the human-capital approach; (2) understanding the case for standardized assessment; (3) understanding the reliability and validity of generic-skills assessment (with evidence from the Collegiate Learning Assessment and the CLA+); (4) understanding the main barriers that need to be overcome; and (5) reframing the uses of generic-skills tests (i.e., understanding the current benefits of generic-skills assessment, and their important new uses).

The five topics are designed as building blocks that fit together. This chapter focuses solely on why the measurement of student learning is essential to understanding the larger topic of academic quality.

1. The primary focus of the human-capital approach (the knowledge, experience, and skills of a nation's citizenry) today is on generic skills, which justifies linking these two concepts together to form the premise for the full argument.

Assessing Quality in Postsecondary Education: International Perspectives, edited by Harvey P. Weingarten, Martin Hicks, and Amy Kaufman. Montréal and Kingston: McGill-Queen's University Press, Queen's Policy Studies Series. © 2018 The School of Policy Studies, Queen's University at Kingston. All rights reserved.

2. While classroom-based assessments of undergraduates by instructors remain central, measurement scientists argue that any assessment with stakes attached requires comparisons. In turn, this also requires standardized assessments that are known to be reliable—given to students under the same conditions and within the same time period.

3. The reliability and validity evidence of the CLA+, a measure of generic skills, appears to be a positive case in point (ETS and ACT also field tests of generic skills seen as reliable and valid).

4. The fact that third-party standardized assessments are not welcomed by many department-based faculty should be a concern. This means reliable and valid comparisons are not possible. If standardized assessments were part of a larger suite of academic disciplines that embraced the value system of science, and were relevant to understanding academic quality, including student learning, that might change the situation. Faculty might then be more positive about third-party-based research, including standardized assessment, which is governed by the principles of transparency, peer review, and the ability to replicate results.

5. If these arguments for standardized assessments and, in particular, generic-skills tests make sense, there are important uses of this test within the university. Equally, there are also new interdisciplinary and global roles for the tests.

The Link Between the Human-Capital Approach and Generic Skills

Gary Becker and his colleagues in the economics department at the University of Chicago get credit for the human-capital approach (Becker 1993). These scholars define human capital as the stock of knowledge and skills present in a nation's population. Such capital accrues through education, training, and experience. As the human-capital field matured, economists began to mine its implications for education (Kreidl, Ganzeboom, and Treiman 2014). The analysis of the returns on the amount and quality of education achieved has become an important research program.

This body of research suggests that education should focus on the knowledge, skills, and experience required in the knowledge economy and society. This means focusing on the ability to access and structure information, and applying it to solve new problems (Simon 1996). Recent theories of learning reflect this change in emphasis from specific content domains to a focus on being able to find and use information. Bransford, Brown, and Cocking (2000) agree that the goal now is to help students develop the intellectual tools and learning strategies needed to acquire the knowledge to think productively. All societies must ensure that their workforce can generate value-added ideas, which can be a foundation for sustained economic growth and prosperity. These skills are seen as requisites for success in the workplace by college graduates. Therefore, this means teaching critical-thinking skills and measuring students' progress toward desired attainment levels. In today's knowledge economy, this privileges the ability to access, structure, and use information, which, in turn, places the focus on generic skills.

The Case for Standardized Assessments

Measurement scientists who work in the education assessment space have developed criteria to evaluate assessment protocols. They are particularly concerned about reliability and validity. Validity is about the extent to which the assessment measures the knowledge, skills, and abilities it was designed to measure. Reliability refers to the degree of consistency of students' (or schools') scores across different assessors, and whether the assessments are given to students under the same conditions and over the same time period. The need for standardized assessments rests on the premise that decisions with stakes attached should be seen to be reliable and valid. If the assessment is not reliable and valid, how can stakeholders rely upon the test results when making decisions with consequences? For example, faculty understandably support student portfolios (Banta and Pike 2012; Rhodes 2012; AAC&U 2005). However, most measurement scientists are skeptical of the claim that portfolios are equal to, or better than, standardized assessments because they have doubts about the reliability of portfolio-based assessments. I share their view and argue that any decision with stakes attached should use a standardized test along with, or in addition to, formative assessments.

What, then, are the major differences between standardized and formative assessments? Perhaps the central distinction between the two groups concerns the different assumption about what unit and level of analysis is appropriate for educational assessment. Adherents of formative assessment privilege the classroom and individual universities as the unit and level of analysis to focus on. They do not believe comparisons between and among universities are possible or, in any event, necessary because they do not believe in standardized tests, and/or they do not believe it is possible to provide interuniversity comparisons. For example, one argument that is frequently expressed is that missions of colleges and universities are so different that it makes no sense to compare them. Furthermore, it is argued that research has shown no statistical differences between institutions on measures of critical thinking, which is the educational component measured most often (Banta and Pike 2012). The second often repeated argument is that variance is much higher within institutions than between institutions, so between-institution comparison is not worth doing (Kuh 2007, 32–3). There are two responses to these assertions.

The first is that most higher-education institutions commit to improving generic skills as a fundamental part of their compact with students. This commitment is enshrined in mission and vision statements of most colleges and universities. Second, the fact that there can be at least two standard deviations among similarly situated colleges and universities, including selective colleges on the CLA+ value-added protocol, means there is a substantial canvas of similar institutions where researchers may study best practices in teaching and learning (Benjamin 2008).

Finally, it has been argued for some time that including performance assessments would encourage greater coherence between instruction, curriculum, assessment, and the complex decision-making tasks faced in life beyond the classroom.

Reliability and Validity Evidence of One Generic-Skills Measure: CLA+

Reliability

The Cronbach's alpha measures the internal consistency of a set of test items. The reliability coefficients for two forms of the CLA+ assessment (one performance task and twenty-five selected-response questions) are .87 (form A) and .85 (form B). These scores are reliable enough for making decisions about grading, admissions, placement, scholarships, etc. (Zahner and James 2015). The reliability coefficient for CLA+ has been at or above .87 in four annual testing administrations, including 2017–18 and also in two test administrations of Teco, the Italian version of CLA+.

Second, CLA+ results can be compared within and between colleges. For example, value-added models can be used to estimate the growth in learning between freshmen and senior-year students. The average effect size reflecting differences in CLA+ performance between entering freshmen and graduating seniors has been .75 over several annual test administrations. There are significant intra- and inter-variations in the effectiveness of efforts to develop generic skills. Going to college matters a good deal and where students go to college is highly significant (Benjamin 2014).

Validity

Construct validity refers to the degree to which test scores may be interpreted as indicators of the particular skills (or construct). Construct validity is often evaluated by examining the patterns of correlations between (or among) a test and similar or different tests. In a technical validity study that carried out this kind of analysis by comparing the tests of critical-thinking skills fielded nationally (e.g., ETS, ACT, and CAE), construct validity for all three tests was demonstrated (Klein et al 2009).[1]

Are Generic Skills Independent?

In a summary of a number of studies, I find that generic skills are applicable over an array of academic disciplines, and can be both assessed and improved by teaching. CLA+ is based on the belief, supported by research, that learning is highly situated and context bound. However, through practice in one subject area, learned knowledge becomes sufficiently generalized to enable students to transfer it to the realm of enhanced reasoning, problem solving, and decision making that can be demonstrated across content domains.

One additional validity question concerns the test paradigm itself. Multiple-choice assessments remain the dominant testing regime. There is a significant education reform movement underway in the United States in both the kindergarten to Grade 12 and the postsecondary sectors. First, there is a shift from the long-standing lecture format to a student-centred approach. Second, there is a change in emphasis in text material, from a primary focus on content to a focus on case studies and problem-based materials. The significant changes underway in these two dimensions of education are ahead of the progress needed in creating assessments that measure the generic skills of students. As-

---

1   Also see Benjamin et al. (2012). Studies of the predictive validity of CLA+ include Steedle (2012), and Zahner and James (2015).

sessments that are better able to measure how well students are learning—and how well institutions are teaching—these skills have become necessary. If the human-capital school demonstrates the importance of education, the implications of the knowledge economy and recent theories of learning place the focus on improving the generic skills of the next generation of students. These developments create an urgent need to generate and implement a testing paradigm that measures and simulates these skills. That paradigm is performance-based assessment, such as that provided by CLA+. However, one issue inhibiting the introduction of this, or any external-based assessment to US universities, is the department-based governance model that is so critical to the success of the US higher-education system.

Department-Based Barriers to Overcome

Department-based governance means professionals in each field of inquiry organize themselves in departments based on the premise that those qualified in a field of knowledge are equipped to govern themselves and, in turn, to decide which fields of inquiry within their discipline should be covered, what subjects should be taught, who should be hired and promoted, and how students should be taught and assessed. No matter how great their knowledge, skills, and/or accomplishments, outsiders are perceived to lack the shared understanding needed to contribute to these decisions in a meaningful way. Faculty are, therefore, typically not interested in whether their instructional methods produce acceptable results based on independent, third-party assessments. Their interests do not often extend to research findings that question the premise of department-based governance (Benjamin and Carroll 1996).

As a result, department-based governance has led to a two-cultures split within the academy. Too many faculty resist science-based research of higher education. Thus, there is a paucity of empirical research supported by the value system of science. Scholarship that is not based on the value system of science lacks transparency and clear peer-review standards, and does not privilege the value of replication of research results. Without systematic empirically based evidence, it will not be possible to propose, develop, and implement effective remedies to the two-cultures division.[2]

---

2 Ostrom (1972) argued for transparent performance metrics about outcomes and key processes in non-profit institutions that are not clearly subject to the discipline of the

Researchers in cognitive science, macroeconomics and microeconomics, educational assessment, educational technology, and data analytics—to name a few—toil in independent silos, isolated from each other. However, they share a commitment to the logic and strategy of scientific inquiry. The premise of the value system of science, peer review,, transparency, and the ability to replicate results are familiar to faculty and administrators. When paired with a coherent and compelling use-inspired basic research strategy, it is possible to imagine a more integrated, interdisciplinary, scientific approach to the challenges that higher education faces.

Framing the Uses of Generic-Skills Tests

The following statement from the "Revised Scoping Paper for an AHELO Main Study" (2015) provides the challenge to which we need to respond: "In a globalizing world, governments want to have more profound knowledge about the education and skills pool at the upper end of the distribution. Economic arguments relating to productivity, innovation, competitiveness and growth, and social arguments relating to social cohesion, trust and various other social outcomes of education create a need for governments to assess the learning outcomes of their new cohorts of tertiary graduates" (OECD 2015, 8).

Current Uses of Generic-Skills Assessment: The CLA+ Case

If leaders of colleges and universities are indeed at a tipping point—simultaneously facing rising costs, declining resources, and a decline in the quality of student-learning outcomes—new decision-making tools that assist college leaders in responding to this challenge would be useful and welcome. CLA+ attempts to provide one decision-making tool for this purpose. The following practical uses of the CLA+ generic-skills assessment, in the form of reports and data analytics offered to all test takers, are designed to assist the higher-education sector improve the quality of student learning, and anchor interdisciplinary research conducted by researchers from the disciplines noted above. Because researchers in all these fields of inquiry share a commitment to the value system of science, which privileges peer review, the ability to

---

market. Simply putting the spotlight on performance indicators causes changes in attitudes and behaviour of the participants, in this case higher-education institutions. This is an example of what Mayo (1949, pp. 60–77) called the Hawthorne Effect.

replicate research results, and public transparency of those results, department-based faculty should be reassured that the results are not controlled or manipulated by policy makers or administrators privately.[3]

Participants in CLA+ receive test results with student, institution, region, and country-based reports with:

- Value-added results
- Certificates/badges with test results for qualifying students (students at the proficient-to-accomplished end of the distribution of generic skills) to showcase their levels of mastery to employers (CLA+ CareerConnect)
- Online results analysis tool, CLA+ Analytics, part of CLA+ Data Miner
- Online videos and interactive exercises to help students improve their generic skills
- Professional development seminars to train professors on the techniques to improve their students' performance

These applications are designed to do the following:

- Permit employers to more easily identify students of high ability who warrant interviews for high, value-added jobs
- Permit graduating seniors to distinguish the level of generic skills they have attained from that of other students
- Permit universities to identify departments and programs that contribute the most to the growth and attainment of generic skills
- Permit ministries of education to identify universities that produce the most value-added growth and/or the highest level of attainment of generic skills
- Permit graduating secondary-school students and their parents to know the level of value-added growth their potential choice of university produces
- Provide the basis for research to understand the impact of resources on the value-added growth, and the highest attainment levels universities provide their students

---

3 Because of the importance of human capital, local, state, and national public leaders are likely to increase their interest in holding institutions accountable for the student-learning results they achieve. Of course, there is considerable debate about whether assessment results should be used for accountability purposes versus improvement. If the faculty and institutions do not have a credible voice in this debate, the department-based barriers will likely continue (Benjamin and Klein 2006, 19).

- Permit researchers to evaluate which academic disciplines contribute the most to student learning-outcomes success
- Provide diagnostic information about the generic skills of entering students, and the retention and graduation rates of students from various demographic backgrounds, in particular under-represented groups
- Provide the basis for cross-national comparisons of similarly situated students, universities, and national systems

Potential Uses and Interdisciplinary Roles of the Generic-Skills Measure

We know from the history of the development of empirical, evidence-based research in agricultural- and health-policy research that there can be an evolution from specific evidence-based results to major new research programs.[4] The question is whether the time is right for a similar transition to occur in higher-education policy research. Two immediate possibilities present themselves.

The decline of productivity growth is an important puzzle to solve. Productivity, defined as the output per hour worked, adjusts for the contribution of capital and materials, and provides a measure of the pace of technological change by tracking productivity growth year over year. From 1948 to 1973 the annual average growth in US productivity declined from 2.5 percent to a stabilized rate of about 1.01 percent in the past decade.[5]

Why does this productivity slowdown, which appears to be similar for other advanced economies, matter? Little or no productivity growth for one or two years is not especially noteworthy. However, annualized year-over-year productivity growth is essential to a national economy and society. Lower economic growth accelerates the rise in social and economic inequality, which appears to be a growing problem in advanced economies today (Piketty 2014). To examine the possible explanations of the slowdown in productivity growth, two subfields of eco-

---

4 Hayami and Ruttan (1987) showed that as a result of the progress in scientific research on agriculture, agricultural economists were able to measure agricultural productivity growth. Following the Flexner Report (Flexner 1910), leaders of medical education decided to change medicine from a clinical to a science-based field.

5 The US permits the most extensive post–World War II historical period to measure productivity growth in advanced economies. Other advanced economies in Western Europe and Asia did not fully recover economically until the mid-1950s. However, OECD-based measures of productivity growth for these countries now presents similar trends to the US.

nomics appear most relevant for our purposes. They are both focused on the service sector.

The first subfield, returns to tertiary education, shows a net decline in the benefits of a BA degree. Kreidl et al. (2014),[6] reviewing occupational trends in education over labour force entry cohorts in forty-two nations over most of the twentieth century and the beginning of the twenty-first century, find that occupational returns to education have been steadily decreasing (Abel and Deitz 2014) .

The second possible explanation is an error in measuring the productivity of the service sector. If we could more accurately measure the service sector (e.g., health, social, and education), productivity growth would look much better. The OECD defines the service economy as "…a diverse group of economic activities, not directly associated with manufacture of goods, mining or agriculture. They typically involve the provision of human value added in the form of labor, advice, managerial skill, entertainment, training, intermediation and the like" (OECD 2000, 7).

Powell and Snellman state that the rise of the service economy involves "…a shift in focus from the principal production and consumption of physical goods to today's principal focus on the production and consumption of services, in particular … knowledge intensive activities" (Powell and Snellman 2004, 199). Nordhaus writes, "… the structural shift from high to low productivity growth sectors, from manufacturing to services)" is the most important contributor to slowing productivity growth, which requires further careful examination (Nordhaus 2016, 3).

The service sector now accounts for over 80 percent of the GDP of the United States and more than 70 percent in OECD member countries overall. Baily and Montalbano argue "…if productivity growth were more accurately measured, particularly in health, education and other services, the growth rate would look better than [it does] currently" (Baily and Montalbano 2016; see also Sprague 2017). This a reasonable position, which leads to the need to re-conceptualize the way we measure GDP. A generic-skills measure could be used to track the productivity growth year over year.

---

6 Other explanations of declining productivity growth include a) mismanagement of new information-technology advances, b) impact of artificial intelligence on investment, c) decline in investment, and d) slowdown in global trade due to national populism.

The OECD Findings Regarding the Skills Mismatch Problem

A generic-skills measure could also illuminate trends in the current debate over a skills mismatch. Is there evidence of a skill mismatch? The OECD finds that more than 40 percent of European workers feel their skill levels do not correspond to those required to do their job. In parallel, many employers report that they face recruitment problems due to skill shortages. "The costs of persistent mismatches and shortages are substantial. For instance, skill shortages can constrain the ability of firms to innovate and adopt new technologies while skill mismatches reduce labour productivity due to the misallocation of workers to jobs. Individuals are also affected as skills mismatch can bring about a higher risk of unemployment, lower wages, lower job satisfaction and poorer career prospects" (OECD 2016a, 7; see also Bol 2015).

In the language of economics, this description is labelled as a maldistribution of human capital at the national level. This statement also describes the impact of a skills mismatch on individuals, which translates as a problem of unequal opportunities for individuals. Since the equality of individual opportunity is a fundamental tenet of liberal democracies, this is also a major policy issue that most, if not all, countries must be concerned with (Benjamin 2016).

The OECD divides skills valued in every job, occupation, and sector into (a) cognitive and non-cognitive skills, and (b) job-specific skills such as technical knowledge associated with a job or occupation (i.e., practical competencies). Key cognitive skills are critical thinking, problem solving, qualitative and quantitative reasoning, and writing mechanics and persuasiveness. Non-cognitive skills refer to persistence, teamwork, entrepreneurial ability, and moral or ethical reasoning ability. While it is recognized that non-cognitive skills are important, it is also recognized that they are not yet measured in a reliable and valid way. Therefore, the immediate focus is on cognitive skills (OECD 2016b).

Experts at the OECD offer two alternatives for moving the cognitive generic-skills agenda forward:

1. Create a comprehensive qualifications framework that would cover all jobs. The challenge here is the need to constantly update changes in each occupation, and make sure that the occupations compared across countries are defined in the same way. The OECD experts recognize this alternative is complex, requires

intensive, large-scale labour, and is cumbersome.[7]

2. The second alternative is to "focus on developing generic or general skills in the education and training system so that workers can more readily adapt to different working environments and allow them to learn field- or job-specific skills in the job" (Montt 2015, 40).

This second alternative is aligned with, and supports, the rationale for focusing on generic skills. The problem, then, is whether we can advance our understanding of both the productivity growth issue and the skills mismatch problem by exploring the potential linkages between them.

The first task is to see whether declining productivity growth supports a closer look at the skills mismatch problem. Second, is there a compelling rationale to introduce a generic-skills assessment to assist efforts to improve measurement of productivity, and aid research that attempts to explain economic growth, the skills mismatch problem, and the increasing inequality of individual opportunity in the workplace? If the generic-skills measurement supports the argument that there is a connection between productivity growth and the skills mismatch issue, this would also demonstrate an absence of a level playing field for many students at the high end of the distribution of generic skills.

Conclusion

The logic of the human-capital approach in today's knowledge economy privileges critical-thinking skills. The focus on the importance of generic skills in today's knowledge economy, which favours the service sector, provides the fundamental rationale for exploration of a new interdisciplinary role for measuring generic skills. First, a generic-skills measure may be used as additional information to track the growth of productivity year over year. Second, the measure may illuminate the trends in the skills mismatch space.

In addition to the current and potential uses of generic-skills measures such as CLA+, quality-assurance agencies are interested in student learning-outcome measures that clearly demonstrate whether the quality of student learning is improving. Because of the problematic history of efforts to develop accountability systems that compel univer-

---

7   A precedent for this in the United States is ACT's Work Keys, a comprehensive map of thousands of vocations.

sities and colleges to demonstrate the level of student learning attained by their graduating seniors, at least in the United States, it may be preferable to focus on measuring the generic skills of a representative sample of graduating seniors within a state, region, or country. This method is more likely to obtain a more statistically accurate picture of what the level of student learning for graduating seniors has reached on an annual basis. The National Assessment of Educational Progress (NAEP) represents one model for such an approach.

The premise of this approach differs from that of the current uses of CLA+ noted above. Instead of using the institution of higher education as the unit of analysis, the student is the focus. The advantage of this approach is that it bypasses the institution altogether. See "An Overview of the NAEP" for a description of this approach, which has become the gold standard for the assessment of the quality of elementary and secondary education in the United States (NAEP 2017). However, since individual universities would not be initially involved in this approach, quality-assurance groups would need to engage the colleges and universities to review the generic-skills assessment results for their state or region to understand the diagnostic results of the assessment, and provide compelling evidence about the level of student learning skills reached by graduating seniors at their institution. The quality-assurance agency might then request that the institution propose changes to its curriculum and pedagogy to improve its student learning results to meet the state or regional requirements set by the quality-assurance agency. In such a model, the quality-assurance agency might recommend the best practices to improve writing, quantitative and qualitative reasoning, and problem solving, (which are core sub-components of generic skills) to levels negotiated between the institutional leaders and the representatives of the quality-assurance agency. The quality-assurance agency might also provide various positive incentives or negative sanctions to encourage the desired improvements.

Finally, the only way to find out whether the generic-skills measure proves to be a useful additional indicator of the productivity growth and skills mismatch issues is to try it out using a number of pilot programs. The proposition put forward here is that a collegiate measure of educational progress, C-NAEP, could serve as the generic-skills measure used to evaluate changes in the skills mismatch problem and the production growth issue.

References

AAC&U (Association of American Colleges & Universities). 2005. *Liberal Education Outcomes: A Preliminary Report on Student Achievement in College*. Washington, DC: Association of American Colleges and Universities.

Abel, Jaison R., and Richard Deitz. 2014. *Do the Benefits of College Still Outweigh the Cost?* Current Issues in Economics and Finance, Vol 20, No. 3. New York: Federal Reserve Bank of New York. https://www.newyorkfed.org/medialibrary/media/research/current_issues/ci20-3.pdf

Baily, Martin, and Nicholas Montalbano. 2016. *Why Is U.S. Productivity Growth So Slow? Possible Explanations and Policy Responses*. Hutchins Center Working Paper No. 22. Washington, DC: The Brookings Institution.

Banta, Trudy W., and Gary Pike. 2012. "Making the Case Against—One More Time." *The Seven Red Herrings about Standardized Assessments in Higher Education*. National Institute of Learning Outcomes. Occasional Paper 15. September: 24–30. http://cae.org/images/uploads/pdf/The_Seven_Red_Herrings_About_Standardized_Assessment_in_Higher_Education.pdf

Becker, Gary. 1993. *Human Capital: A Theoretical and Empirical Analysis with Special Reference to Education*, 2nd ed. Chicago: University of Chicago Press.

Benjamin, Roger. 2008. "The Case for Comparative Institutional Assessment of Higher-Order Thinking Skills." *Change: The Magazine of Higher Learning* 40 (6): 15–21.

———. 2014. "Two Questions about Critical-Thinking Tests in Higher Education." *Change: The Magazine of Higher Learning* 46 (2): 32–9.

———. 2016. *Leveling the Playing Field from College to Career*. New York: Council for Aid to Education. http://cae.org/images/uploads/pdf/Leveling_the_Playing_Field_From_College_To_Career.pdf

Benjamin, Roger, and Stephen J. Carroll. 1996. "Impediments and Imperatives in Restructuring Higher Education." *Educational Administration Quarterly* 32 (1): 705–19.

Benjamin, Roger, and Stephen Klein. 2006. *Assessment versus Accountability: Notes for Reconciliation*. UNESCO Occasional Paper No. 2. Paris: UNESCO.

Benjamin, Roger, Stephen Klein, Jeffrey Steedle, Doris Zahner, Scott Elliot, and Julie Patterson. 2012. *The Case for Generic Skills in the United States and International Settings*. New York: Council for Aid to Education. http://cae.org/images/uploads/pdf/The_Case_for_Generic_Skills_ and_Performance_Assessment.pdf

Bol, Thijs. 2015. "Has Education Become More Positional? Educational Expansion and Labour Market Outcomes, 1985–2007." *Acta Sociologica*, 58 (2): 105–20.

Bransford, John, Anthony Brown, and Robert Cocking. 2000. *How People Learn: Brain, Mind, Experience, and School*. Washington, DC: National Academy Press.

Flexner, Abraham. 1910. *Medical Education in the United States and Canada: A Report to the Carnegie Foundation for the Advancement of Teaching*. New York: The Carnegie Foundation for the Advancement of Teaching, Bulletin No. 4.

Hayami, Yujiro, and Vernon W. Ruttan. 1987. *Agricultural Development: An International Perspective*. 2nd ed. Baltimore: Johns Hopkins University Press.

Klein, Stephen, Lydia Liu, James Sconing, Roger Bolus, Brent Bridgeman, Brent, Heather Kugelmass, Alexander Nemeth, Steven Robbins, and Jeffrey Steedle. 2009. *Test Validity Study Report*. Fund for the Improvement of Postsecondary Education, U.S. Department of Education. https://cp-files.s3.amazonaws.com/26/TVSReport_Final.pdf

Kreidl, Martin, Harry B. G. Ganzeboom, and Donald J. Treiman. 2014. *How Did Occupational Returns To Education Change Over Time?* Los Angeles: California Center for Population Research, University of California, Los Angeles. http://citeseerx.ist.psu.edu/viewdoc/download?-doi=10.1.1.661.8511&rep=rep1&type=pdf

Kuh, George. 2007. "Risky Business: Promises and Pitfalls of Institutional Transparency." *Change* 29 (5): 30–5.

Mayo, Elton. 1949. *Hawthorne and the Western Electric Company. The Social Problems of Industrial Civilization*. London: Routledge.

Montt, Guillermo. 2015. *The Causes and Consequences of Field-of-Study Mismatch: An Analysis Using PIAAC*. OECD Social, Employment and Migration Working Papers, No. 167. Paris: OECD Publishing.

NAEP (National Assessment of Educational Progress). 2017. *An Overview of NAEP*. Washington, DC: Center for Education Statistics, United States Department of Education. https://nces.ed.gov/nationsreport card/subject/_commonobjects/pdf/2013455.pdf

Nordhaus, William D. 2016. "Why Growth Will Fall." *The New York Review of Books*. 18 August: 1–3. http://www.nybooks.com/articles/ 2016/08/18/why-economic-growth-will-fall/

Piketty, Thomas. 2014. *Capital in the Twenty-First Century*. Translated by

Arthur Goldhammer. Cambridge: Harvard University Press.

Powell, Walter W., and Kaisa Snellman. 2004. "The Knowledge Economy." *Annual Review of Sociology* 30 (1): 199–220.

OECD (Organisation for Economic Co-operation and Development). 2000. *The Service Economy*. Business and Industry Policy Forum Series. Paris: OECD Publishing. https://www.oecd.org/sti/ind/2090561.pdf

———. 2015. *Revised Scoping Paper For An AHELO Main Study*. Directorate for Education and Skills. Paris: OECD Publishing.

———. 2016a. *Getting Skills Right: Assessing and Anticipating Changing Skill Needs*. Paris: OECD Publishing. http://www.keepeek.com/Digital-Asset-Management/oecd/employment/getting-skills-right-assessing-and-anticipating-changing-skill-needs_9789264252073-en#.WeTQAFtSxhE

———. 2016b. *Skills Matter: Further Results from the Survey of Adult Skills*. Paris: OECD Publishing. http://www.keepeek.com/Digital-Asset-Management/oecd/education/skills-matter_9789264258051-en#.WeTQQFtSxhE

Ostrom, Vincent. 1972. "Polycentricity." Paper presented at the annual meeting of the American Political Science Association, Washington, DC, September.

Rhodes, Terrel. 2012. "Getting Serious About Assessing Authentic Student Learning." *The Seven Red Herrings about Standardized Assessments in Higher Education*. National Institute of Learning Outcomes. Occasional Paper 15. September: 19–23. http://www.learningoutcomes assessment.org/documents/HerringPaperFINAL1.pdf

Simon, Herbert. 1996. *The Sciences of the Artificial*. Boston: MIT Press.

Sprague, Shawn. 2017. "Below Trend: The U.S. Productivity Slowdown Since the Great Recession." *Beyond the Numbers: Productivity*, Vol. 6, No. 2. Bureau of Labor Statistics. January. https://www.bls.gov/opub/btn/volume-6/below-trend-the-us-productivity-slowdown-since-the-great-recession.htm

Steedle, Jeffrey T. 2012. "Selecting Value-Added Models for Postsecondary Institutional Assessment." *Assessment & Evaluation in Higher Education*, 37 (6): 637–52.

Zahner, Doris, and Jessalynn K. James. 2015. *Predictive Validity of a Critical Thinking Assessment for Post-College Outcomes*. New York: Council for Aid to Education. 30 September.

Section II

Europe

4

Governance and Power Through Indicators: The UK Higher Education Teaching Excellence and Student Outcomes Framework

Roger King

Introduction

The Teaching Excellence and Student Outcomes Framework (TEF), introduced in 2016 by the UK government for universities and colleges, may be regarded as an extension of the performance-measures culture that has enveloped most other UK public service organizations and that highlights the desirability of value-for-money calculations in achieving outcomes on behalf of taxpayers and consumers.

Although the TEF is intended to cover the four countries of the UK, albeit with different emphases, the focus of this chapter is on England, which offers the most advanced rollout of the scheme. Moreover, the explicit link between TEF outcomes and tuition fee increases is found only in England.

A performance culture has become well-established in higher education in England—but for research. For nearly three decades, the Higher Education Funding Council for England (HEFCE)—and its predecessor bodies—has operated the highly successful Research Excellence Frame-

Assessing Quality in Postsecondary Education: International Perspectives, edited by Harvey P. Weingarten, Martin Hicks, and Amy Kaufman. Montréal and Kingston: McGill-Queen's University Press, Queen's Policy Studies Series. © 2018 The School of Policy Studies, Queen's University at Kingston. All rights reserved.

work (REF) on behalf of the government. This scheme evaluates the comparative research performance of individual academics and their universities, and then distributes research funding selectively on the basis of these evaluations.

Not only has the REF proved to be a highly effective resources distribution formula (the original policy intention), it has come to be regarded as raising the overall quality of the research effort and output through its competitive dynamics, and as contributing to the high status of UK universities. If teaching and learning need to be seen as equal to research—as many argue—it cannot be on the basis that research is performance-managed and teaching is not. Performance measures have driven up quality in research and the TEF aims to do the same for teaching. However, this will only happen if the TEF truly measures teaching excellence in the metrics that have been adopted. Critics argue that the TEF does not create a plausible relationship to teaching that would enable it to support the enhancement of teaching quality. Its proxies (indicators) for teaching excellence are the subject of considerable controversy.

Arguably, the success of the REF has reinforced the relatively lower standing of teaching and learning in UK higher education. It has proved difficult to conduce a similar competitive and open-market-like system to enable incentives and rewards to flow to where the highest teaching and learning quality is located. In comparison with research, external teaching evaluation has proved elusive. Teaching's authenticity is still derived from subject experience and research. The rise of wired classrooms and the availability of big data may in time enable wider external assessment. For now, the TEF suffices.

The TEF matters to the UK government. An increasing government focus on students as fee-paying consumers, and as being at the "heart of the system," has meant that raising the performance and standing of teaching and learning (to that of research, if possible) has become a policy imperative. The TEF is an attempt to find a similar scheme to that of the research-funding programs to deliver on these purposes, not least by providing student consumers with more informed knowledge and choice.

Formally, the government outlines four key purposes of the TEF:

1. Better informing students' choices about where and what to study
2. Raising esteem for teaching
3. Recognizing and rewarding excellent teaching

4. Better meeting the needs of employers, business, industry, and the professions

In England, with the exception of the Open University (which claimed it was too distinctive in its data profile and teaching delivery to be the subject of an accurate TEF evaluation), there were no significant university omissions in the applications for the TEF year two exercise. In Scotland, where there is no devolved government policy directly supporting the TEF (and with vocal critics such as the University of Edinburgh), five universities entered the TEF scheme for year two (winning three gold and two silver awards). In Wales, Aberystwyth and the University of South Wales were missing, while in Northern Ireland the two leading universities—Queen's University Belfast and the University of Ulster—did not participate (although two others did).

Although year one of the scheme began in 2016 with a transitional set of arrangements and pilots, effectively it was in year two (2016–17) that the program was more fully implemented. Although confined to undergraduate awards (and equivalent qualifications), it is the government's intention that in future TEFs, postgraduate studies, and analysis by subjects (not just whole institutions) will be included. While a postgraduate TEF is not immediately on the government's horizon, a subject-level piloting exercise will start in 2018.

The UK Department for Education sets the specification for the TEF (and determines any fee and loan increases that are allowed arising from the TEF outcomes), while HEFCE, working with the Quality Assurance Agency (QAA), has been asked to implement the scheme. (HEFCE is being merged into, and will be supplanted by, a new sector-wide regulator, the Office for Students. This was scheduled to start in January 2018.)

The TEF and Governing by Indicators

The TEF is an example of indicators as an emerging technology in the practice of governance. Various aggregations of indicators, such as indexes, rankings, and composites are included in our description of indicators as a governance technology. These are often mashed-up compilations with considerable choice available to the progenitors in deciding which particular indicators to choose, the levels of weightings, and the methods to mitigate double counting or to overcome data unavailability. Often these composites are readily transformed into numerical data.

The simplification methodology used for compiling indicators includes means for aggregating data from many sources—and excluding other data not deemed to be reliable or representative. That is, the organization and simplification of the data generally is taken to denote the essence of the social phenomenon represented by the data. In the case of the TEF, teaching excellence is taken as being evidenced by data collected from a number of different sources, which is then integrated and subsequently categorized into different standards of performance—bronze, silver, and gold.

Although these broader categorizations in the TEF, rather than precise rank-ordered institutional scores, may facilitate initial acceptance of the scheme, it may store up trouble for later. There is evidence that institutions find it more difficult in reputation terms to deal with dropping a category (from excellent to good, for example) than with relatively marginal shifts in overall scores over time. That is, a small or incremental change in a TEF score may lead to a quite public drop in a category—from, say, gold to silver—that may appear to be quite catastrophic at least in public-relations (and possibly tuition-fee) terms.

Moreover, although institutions may resubmit to the TEF annually, it is not clear why those with gold and silver awards would take the risk and incur the expenditure to do so rather than wait for the mandated three-year cycle. Consequently, there may not be much change in the rankings in the early years at least (rather defeating the purpose of stimulating institutions to improve their performances). If TEF-linked differential tuition-fee benefits kick in (as proposed, after 2020), diminishing funds may make investment for securing TEF improvement difficult to find for some institutions. One-word indicators such as gold, silver, and bronze may in time come to be regarded as being too rigid to incentivize the changes in institutional teaching performance that the TEF is intended to generate.

Indicators such as the TEF respond to demands for (and receptivity to) numerical, rank-ordered, and comparable data—that is, to the desire to make visible or legible that which is difficult to know publicly. Such indicators seek to turn an activity (such as classroom teaching) and its outcomes that are rather secretive and invisible, into something more transparent, accountable, and capable of being evaluated. A key assumption, of course, is that indicators reflect the phenomenon they purport to measure, albeit in a simplified form.

Although considerable controversy often attends these claims to simplified representation, it is the very reductionism that underlies the appeal of indicators to both consumers and policy makers. They are intended to be convenient and easy to understand. Numerical data appears to possess technical neutrality and objectivity, in comparison with the more complicated and nuanced accounts provided by insiders. Moreover, as Davis et al. note, "They are often numerical representations of complex phenomena intended to render these simple and more comparable with other complex phenomena, which have also been represented numerically" (Davis et al. 2012, 8). As such, "indicators can conceal nuances and restrict contestation by displacing subjective decision making with the appearance of hard data" (Fisher 2012, 217).

Of course, controversies over indicators focus often on the "exclusion of narrative" (Espeland 2015), or stripping away of context and meaning for the numeric representations. In a sense, the stark comparisons of indicators, excluding ambiguity, but using often flawed data or data collected for other purposes, "absorbs uncertainty" in the processes of categorization. Porter (1995) similarly argues that quantifications are "thinning practices" that do not systematically supplant deeper, narrative forms of knowing, which he calls "thickening practices." Rather, the two practices are suited to diverse circumstances and evolve in the dynamic relationships between localizing and universalizing tendencies.

The thinning practices associated with indicators and their underlying data, in a sense, reflect similar patterns within the authority structures of the organizations tasked with collecting and submitting data on themselves that is used by external compilers to evaluate their performances. It is worth quoting from Espeland and Stevens on these processes: "Raw information typically is collected and compiled by workers near the bottom of organizational hierarchies; but as it is manipulated, parsed, and moved upward, it is transformed so as to make it accessible and amenable for those near the top, who make the big decisions. This editing removes assumptions, discretions, and ambiguity…Information appears more robust than it actually is…The premises behind the numbers disappear, with the consequence that decisions seem more obvious than they might otherwise have been. An often unintended effect of this phenomenon is numbers that appear more authoritative as they move up a chain of command. The authority of the information parallels the authority of its handlers in the hierarchy" (Espeland and Stevens 2008, and quoted in Davis et al. 2012, 8).

Clearly, indicators contain statements or models of standards against which performance or conduct is measured. In conceptualizing an indicator initially, an underlying explanation for change is assumed. This involves a theory, the construction of categories for measurement, and modes of data analysis. For example, when indicators of teaching excellence are formulated, they build on a theory of what is problematic that needs to be overcome by improvements in practice and outcomes The indicator effectively defines what constitutes standards by the assemblage of specific criteria and measurements.

Governing at a Distance

In governance terms, these standards allow authority to be exercised at a distance based on the legibility provided by numeric and similar representations (however simplified) to the governmental centre. In UK higher education, particularly in England, the atomistic nature of individual units (institutions) with responsibility for their own futures and operating both competitively and collaboratively, allows both delegated powers/responsibilities from the state to these (corporately managed) geographically dispersed institutions, while exercising external monitoring and intervention where judged to be necessary.

These large networks of independent agents produce the data required by compilers, including government. In the case of the TEF, the state lends its authority or brand (and resources), but without being the primary determinant of its content. As the awareness and significance of the TEF indicators rise, its design is likely to become the subject of contestation, with demands for greater transparency, input, reason-giving, and review. Responding to such demands, compilers typically highlight their claims that indicators are efficient, consistent, open, scientific, neutral, and cost-effective.

Moreover, increased data availability, cheaper and higher-powered computers, and improvements in statistical techniques allow quite rapid communications with stakeholders when they inquire further into the data's complexities and limitations. Unlike more traditional political forms of power contestation, so-called technical experts—those with expertise in the analysis of indicators—become particularly influential. Over time, as indicators such as the TEF become established, they gather supporters and advocates, as well as technological and related advances, which provide a form of snowball effect. A special power is given to numbers (and rankings) as definitive and simplifying heuristics, and which are highly portable and abstract in contrast to the dense material of long descriptions.

Successful indicators, such as the UK's REF for example, that become institutionalized, produce what Espeland and Sauder (2012, 86) describe as "powerful and unanticipated effects: they can change how people think about what they do," including how excellence is to be defined. Those being evaluated thus "often respond to the act of being measured in ways that subvert the intentions that first motivated the assessment process." Indicators produce a "reactivity" in that indicators prompt intense pressure to change behaviour and improve scores.

In their analysis of law schools, for example, Espeland and Sauder (2012, 89) show that indicators "produce important changes in how schools and applicants behave" as they adapt to the models and standards in the rankings. "Rankings encourage conformity among law schools, in that those devoted to missions not captured by rankings, feel pressure to change those missions." Their prospective students, absent any other simple way to compare schools, or the resources to interrogate them to establish the accuracy of comparisons, are inclined to be less critical of the numbers as establishing real differences.

Other stakeholders too, such as employers, find the convenience of rankings and indicators sufficiently strong to discount methodological and other critical counters from academic staff and policy observers. Moreover, as the indicator becomes taken for granted, the decisions based on the indicator also receive less scrutiny. The number of institutions refusing to participate is likely to decline. Rather, for the lowly ranked, inclusion in an indicator such as the TEF grants visibility and legitimacy as a recognized player in the system. But even for the middle ranked, doing well in the TEF may enable an institution to help differentiate itself from the great mass of mid-table institutions.

It is for these reasons (and others) that the influential Wilsdon Report published in the UK (2015) has been considered important. It argues for "responsible metrics" as a way of framing appropriate uses of quantitative indicators, which is understood in the following dimensions:

- Robustness—basing metrics on the best possible data in terms of accuracy and scope
- Humility—recognizing that quantitative evaluation should support, but not supplant qualitative, expert assessment
- Transparency—keeping data collection and analytical processes open and transparent, so that those being evaluated can test and verify the results
- Diversity—accounting for variation by field, and using a range of indicators to reflect and support a plurality

- Reflexivity—recognizing and anticipating the systemic and potential effects of indicators, and updating them in response

The TEF is likely to dominate the ranking of learning and teaching in England as a powerful single indicator sponsored by the state. As such it will have considerable authority, particularly to outside audiences. Although competitors may arise, it is doubtful that they will have the influence of the TEF. The competitive multiplicity of various rankings and indicators, as found in the world of business schools, for example, will be lacking. As such, the ability of institutional leaders to spin away the TEF to external audiences by pointing them to credible TEF-like alternatives is unlikely to be available.

Rather, the TEF provides a striking example of how quantitative knowledge is used increasingly for governing social life by both governmental and non-governmental bodies. It enables them to distribute attention, make decisions, and allocate scarce resources. As global connections increase, the demand for readily comparable and accessible knowledge escalates as a means of dealing with rapid change and high uncertainty.

Although a justifying argument for such developments is the aid to transparency and democratic accountability, the production of these numeric systems is rarely transparent or public, but confined mainly to experts in quantitative approaches. These constraints are also accompanied by reliance on data that is available, and that is judged to be broadly relevant (proxies). Moreover, this may reflect simply what states and private organizations have decided to collect and quantify for other or very different purposes. The processes of quantification encode particular cultural understandings, political interests, and world views. Those that become successful and have major impacts come to be supported by powerful forces of institutionalization, and by powerful organizations. If indicators work in institutionalized practice they will be accepted as real—it is the institutionalization that makes indicators real rather than any ontological determination. In turn, this creates stabilization.

TEF: Metrics and Operation

In light of previous attempts to evaluate and raise the performance of undergraduate teaching by presenting public awards and similar incentives to lecturers, which have done little to demonstrate an overall rise in standards or relative status for university teaching, the TEF understandably moves away from the direct focus on the teacher. Rather, in the TEF's guidance, teaching quality "is best considered in the context of students' learning. The outcomes of students' learning are determined by the quality of the teaching they experience, the additional support for learning that is available, and what the students put into their studies, supported and facilitated by the provider" (HEFCE 2016). That is, teaching excellence is indicated by student performance and related outcomes.

Essentially, TEF metrics are derived from three existing and updated data collections: the National Student Survey (NSS), which measures students' views on their teaching, assessment, and feedback, and academic support; the annual Higher Education Statistics Agency data collection from institutions (notably on continuation rates); and Student Employment Destination surveys (on employment and further study).

The TEF is a student performance framework that focuses on dimensions of student inputs, processes, and outputs in formulating institutional metrics for evaluation. Thus, teaching excellence is "defined broadly to include teaching quality, the learning environment, student outcomes, and learning gain" (HEFCE 2016).

In November 2016, HEFCE released each provider's metrics to them based on HEFCE records and returns. These metrics are benchmarked for institutions in similar categories (that is, those with similar student population profiles), while both TEF evaluators and institutions are provided with information on institutional contextual factors. Institutions are invited to check, and seek adjustments to their metrics if felt necessary, and then, if meeting the eligibility requirements concerning sufficient core data, apply for a TEF assessment. It is important to note that institutional scores are benchmarked rather than absolute; that is, universities and colleges are judged on how well they do compared to how well they could be expected to do given their institutional profile.

Essentially, providers must have a minimum set of reportable metrics to apply for a TEF rating higher than the lowest of the three successful awards—bronze—as well as usually needing three years of benchmarked data for each of the core metrics. Also, institutions must have an access agreement or a publicly available access statement to be TEF eligible (the former consists of agreed targets for social access intakes made with the Office for Fair Access, or OFFA, although the TEF will accept a published access statement on an institution's website in lieu of an OFFA agreement). TEF metrics include those for overseas students. Data and evaluations apply to those universities and colleges that actually deliver the teaching, under, say, franchise arrangements, rather than, say, the awarding body.

Finally, although the metrics outcomes play a large part in final evaluations, a TEF panel largely drawn from the sector (with recommendations from a wider pool of academic and student assessors) provides, at the end, a holistic judgment. This includes consideration of institutional submissions—of no more than fifteen pages—adding context, explaining performance, putting forward evidence, and exploring performance for specific student groups. Final judgments categorize institutions as gold, silver, or bronze according to evaluated student performance for each institution. Nonetheless, the TEF panel, in formal guidance at least, is restricted in how far it can overlook institutional negatives that are flagged by the metrics (in actuality, these restrictions become more flexible as the TEF panel considers institutional narrative submissions, as we see below).

Benchmarking

For each metric and each provider, full-time and part-time students are reported separately. Further, performance is shown within a number of subgroups (for example, full-time males, part-time domiciled students, ethnicity, disability). To aid the TEF panel, core and split metrics are flagged if they are significantly and materially above or below a weighted-sector average (benchmark).

Benchmarks are used to allow meaningful comparisons between providers by taking into account the different mix of students at each provider. A unique benchmark is calculated for each provider's core and split metrics. The benchmark is a weighted-sector average where weightings are based on the characteristics of the students at the provider. This means that the provider is not being compared to a pre-set group of providers. Each provider has its own benchmark for each core and split metric.

For the purpose of calculating benchmarks, the sector is made up of all providers, regardless of whether they have chosen to enter the TEF. The benchmarking factors for each metric are subject of study, entry qualifications, age on entry, ethnicity, sex, disability, and social disadvantage. These are then profiled against the NSS, non-continuation, employment or further study, and highly skilled employment or further study metrics.

Once the core and split metrics are calculated and benchmarked during the initial phases of a TEF cycle, those results that are significantly and materially different (positive and negative) are highlighted (flagged). The TEF panel assessors use these flags to form an initial judgment of the provider. A provider with three or more positive flags and no negative flags should be considered initially as gold; two or more negatives (regardless of the number of positive flags) as bronze; and everyone else, including those with no flags, as silver.

In the 2016–17 cycle the TEF panel departed significantly in a large number of cases from these initial assessments. However, it is difficult to perceive why as the TEF panel's deliberations were confidential, and it offered only brief summary judgments on each institution at the conclusion of the exercise.

Metrics and Peer Review

Following the announcement in June 2017 of TEF year two awards, it is not clear to what extent evaluations of student performance have been based on metrics, and the extent to which more qualitative peer-based judgments (by the TEF panel) have been influential. As we have noted, on the basis of the metrics, institutional performances were flagged to the TEF panel if they were significantly outside respective award boundaries. Although the flags potentially inhibit more qualitative judgments, there is evidence that the TEF panel felt able to ignore these when it had strong evidence in the institutional contextual submissions to do so. (For example, it may well have underplayed some institution's NSS scores on the grounds that such scores tend to be downgraded in large conurbations, such as London, for reasons that may have little to do with the university attended).

Moreover, there appears to have been quite high variability by institutions in writing their TEF narrative. Some are very data driven while others are more qualitative, and some used committees, small teams, or even external consultants. It would appear that many institutions had difficulty in writing prospectively rather than simply looking back.

In its outcomes published in June 2017, the TEF panel provided short statements for each institution that give some explanation for its conclusions about each provider's award. But these comprise basically bullet points taken from institutional narrative submissions (which are unverified) and whether the panel accepted or not that there was sufficient evidence of successful actions to overcome negative flagging. At first glance, some institutions appear to have benefited more than others from the panel's discretions in having awards upgraded from what had been expected from the institutional metrics alone.

The TEF panel chose to exercise its judgment to overrule the metrics sixty-four times (out of 295 judgments, or 22 percent), including thirty-six times for higher-education institutions and alternative providers. While three institutions had their final assessments downgraded from their initial evaluation, thirty-three institutions had their final assessments upgraded (including eight in the elite Russell Group, from the twenty-one such institutions that entered the TEF—those in England mainly). Further education colleges (which provide technical and professional education and training) with higher-education programs, however, experienced much more general downgrading than the universities.

Overall, excluding provisional awards, 32 percent of the higher-education institutions achieved gold, 50 percent silver, and 18 percent bronze whereas 34 percent of further education colleges received a bronze award (perhaps indicating a relative shortage of resources for handling TEF requirements, particularly for the written submissions). It would appear that six institutions received a gold despite having only one positive flag (some way below the three needed for an initial gold assessment as stated in the initial TEF guidance); four of these were Russell Group institutions. Six universities that received silver awards had at least two negative and no positive flags. The TEF panel interpretations of the narrative submissions may help explain these variations from the assessments provided by the metrics alone, but there is no real evidence available in the public domain to analyze this. As with the REF, the TEF will continue to face contestation of the respective role that metrics and expert, peer, or qualitative judgment should play in these evaluation exercises.

Early planning scenarios by HEFCE had suggested a likely distribution of awards as 20 percent bronze; 20–30 percent gold; and 50–60 percent silver. These expectations proved quite accurate: excluding provisional awards 26 percent (fifty-nine providers) were awarded gold, 50 percent (116 providers) silver, and 24 percent (fifty-six providers) bronze.

At least four institutions appealed their TEF awards, focusing on the use of the narrative method and claims that poor metric scores among institutions were treated differently by the panel. However, providers are only able to appeal on the basis of a significant procedural irregularity and are not able to challenge the underpinning principles of the

TEF or the academic judgment of the panels.

In England, the wholesale participation in the TEF by institutions would appear to have been influenced by the proposed ability (for gold, silver, and bronze recipients) to raise their tuition fees in line with inflation. The falling relative value of the pound sterling after the Brexit referendum has substantially increased inflationary pressures in the UK as import costs become more expensive. Consequently, the potential tuition-fee increase may be considerable, at least in comparison with what would have been likely in the relatively benign inflationary conditions of previous years. A university with around 15,000 students would benefit by around £1 million in 2018, which is considerable, particularly if falling student numbers and / or declining revenue are exerting strong bottom-line pressures.

If differential fee increases tied to TEF outcomes are confirmed after 2020 (after an independent review of the TEF established by government and scheduled for 2019), then substantial financial as well as reputational gains are likely to accrue to those institutions that do well in the TEF. What opportunities bronze, and perhaps some silver, recipients may have over the next cycle to upgrade their performance in time for future three-year assessments is not clear. Although some universities clearly excelled at both the TEF and the REF (Oxford and Cambridge particularly), and some did well in one but not the other (London School of Economics and Political Science in the REF but not the TEF, Coventry in the TEF but not the REF), some institutions, such as London Metropolitan University, did badly in both. Boards of governors and other stakeholders are likely to place managers and staff in such universities under considerable strategic pressure to decide how they wish the university to be taken forward and with what priorities.

In conclusion, the TEF, and a recently reformed quality assurance system, are together intended to form a coherent system for assessing the learning and teaching quality of universities and colleges in England. Both are designed to play distinctive but complementary roles. Primarily, institutional quality assurance is conducted internally (including a larger oversight role by boards of governors) and reported on annually as part of an annual provider review to the external regulator, who will visit the institution every five years or so. In this way, institutions are monitored to see if they meet baseline or threshold standards (explicated by the expectations of the UK Quality Code for Higher Education as applied to date by the QAA; and by QAA's Frameworks for Higher Education Qualifications or its Higher Education Review for alternative providers).

The TEF, however, aims to incentivize excellent teaching above the baseline and provide better information for students to support them in making informed choices. "QAA and TEF will therefore work together to promote, support, and reward continuous improvement and better student outcomes" (HEFCE 2016).

Issues

Among the issues raised by the Teaching Excellence and Student Outcomes Framework and its operational details are the following:

- To what extent does the input, process, and output data indicate some form of teaching excellence or, more broadly, student performance, or are the variables too contingently connected to other factors, such as the strength of local labour markets?
- How likely is it that institutions will learn to game the system, not least in manipulating data submissions, thus making the student performance evaluation provided by the TEF less reliable?
- In light of university rankings' systems, will the TEF act as a disciplinary influence on institutions (particularly if there are major reputational and financial implications for TEF performance), so that internal procedures and processes (and priorities) reflect the external pressures of the TEF rather than the strategic purposes of the university or college?
- Will the TEF determine what teaching excellence means at the expense of other models and elevate its dimensions to overcome alternative interpretations and methods for measuring quality learning environments?
- Will the accumulated fifteen-page submissions or institutional context narratives that appear to have significantly influenced the recent TEF year two outcomes (by way of interpretations from the TEF panel), be subject to a more tightly defined format and be required to be verified and auditable?

There is little doubt that the TEF will be fine-tuned further over coming years, not only through the addition of a subject-based framework, but through more course- and institution-specific data on such issues as future earnings. For example, the graduate premium varies hugely by course and institution, and students need to know more to make informed decisions. The UK government's Longitudinal Education Outcomes project, which uses tax data to investigate graduation earnings, undoubtedly will become incorporated into the TEF in time, not least as the data for all subjects is published.

Resources

As a government initiative, the TEF receives both significant funding as well as authoritative resources in devising indicators and linking them to data. Even so, there is no great additional data collection involved, which can be expensive and time-consuming. Countries seeking to implement similar TEF schemes elsewhere will recognize that governments are required to provide significant input and the bill rises even further if there is little in the way of existing data that can be manipulated for the new task. Which indicators are used and what they measure will vary depending on where the financial support for the initiative comes from. If an indicator is intended for a wide audience (as with the TEF) there is also a necessity to ensure clear and easy formats, as well as conceptual simplicity, and this may be expensive. For the most part, data collected for other purposes will be adapted and used as proxies, which raises technical and political difficulties.

Institutional buy-in is particularly important on legitimacy grounds, but also to ensure that the process of data collection and submission is as effective and as efficient as possible. Nonetheless, there is an incentive when data is collected in this way for the massaging of categories and data without targeted and regular audit. In the absence of independent data gathering, the collection of data can be problematic. It raises the question, what is most important: the problem to be measured or data availability? If the former, there is more likely a need for resources to collect new data rather than adopt what exists.

The TEF uses subjective or qualitative expert opinion and the relationship between this process and the use of metrics is not yet clear and is likely to remain a continuing controversy, involving sector culture, professional autonomy, and methodological difficulties.

Conclusions

The TEF is likely to become a distinct evaluation of UK university performance, for reasons over and above its sponsorship or branding by the state. Unlike nearly all other such rankings and evaluation exercises, research performance and students' entry grades are not used to produce the outcomes. It differs, too, at the moment, in that the TEF provides a judgment of relative rather than absolute performance through its data benchmarking process. The TEF panel took into account differences among institutions, so the final rating recognizes the value added by a university rather than its unvarnished quality.

Whether these features will be retained as the TEF rolls forward and is re-evaluated, and as those elite universities that have performed quite poorly in the TEF year two exercise begin their lobbying of government, is to be seen—as will any impact on prospective students' decision making (UCAS, the university and college central student-admissions system, will mark institutions with their respective TEF year two scores in its material, which may have some influence). The TEF also remains an evaluation of student experience rather than a clear guide to the excellence or otherwise of an institution's teaching. In time, however, increasingly digital classrooms in universities may generate sufficient data to more accurately reveal the quality of a teacher, or a group of teachers, than the TEF is currently able to do.

References

Davis, Kevin, Angelina Fisher, Benedict Kingsbury, and Sally Engle Merry, eds. 2012. *Governance by Indicators: Global Power through Classification and Rankings*. Oxford: Oxford University Press.

Espeland, Wendy. 2015. "Narrating Numbers." In *The World of Indicators: The Making of Governmental Knowledge through Quantification*, edited by Richard Rottenburg, Sally Merry, Sung-Joon Park and Joanna Mugler, 56–75. Cambridge: Cambridge University Press.

Espeland, Wendy, and Michael Sauder. 2012. "The Dynamism of Indicators," In *Governance by Indicators: Global Power through Classification and Rankings*, edited by Kevin Davis, Angelina Fisher, Benedict Kingsbury, and Sally Engle Merry. Oxford: Oxford University Press.

Espeland, Wendy, and Mitchell Stevens. 2008. "A Sociology of Quantification." *European Journal of Sociology* 49 (3), 401–36.

Fisher, A. 2012. "From Diagnosing Under-Immunization to Evaluating Health Care Systems: Immunization Coverage Indicators as a Technology of Global Governance." In *Governance by Indicators: Global Power through Classification and Rankings*, edited by Kevin Davis, Angelina Fisher, Benedict Kingsbury, and Sally Engle Merry, 217–48. Oxford: Oxford University Press.

HEFCE (Higher Education Funding Council for England). 2016. *Teaching Excellence Framework, 2016*.

———. 2017. *Teaching Excellence Framework Year Two: Outcomes 2.*

Porter, Theodore M. 1995. *Trust in Numbers: The Pursuit of Objectivity in Science and Public Life.* Princeton: Princeton University Press.

Wilsdon, James et al. 2015. *The Metric Tide: Report of the Independent Review of the Role of Metrics in Research Assessment and Management.* doi:10.13140/RG 2.1.4929.1363

5

Assessing Teaching and Learning in Ireland[1]

Fergal Costello and Ellen Hazelkorn

Introduction

The governance of Irish higher education has been undergoing significant changes over the last few decades, paralleling the massification of the system and an increasing recognition of its role in Irish society, especially the economy (Walsh 2014a; 2014b). European Union (EU) membership, rapid social and demographic changes, economic growth, foreign direct investment, and international competitiveness have all driven the demand for higher education. Fundamental to this expansion has been the sustained policy emphasis on access to education at increasingly advanced levels, from the introduction of free secondary education in the mid-1960s to free undergraduate education in 1996. Today, there are seven universities and fourteen institutes of technology (IoTs), alongside a small number of other publicly aided institutions; 55 percent of new entrants attend universities and 45 percent attend IoTs. About 80 percent of students are enrolled full time and are within the

---

1 The terminology used throughout this chapter is drawn from Irish regulations and documentation. This can differ from terminology used in Canada. For example, post-secondary is commonly used in Canada; in Ireland, further (vocational and pre-college programmes) and higher education (BA, MA, PhD) are used to distinguish between different components of the tertiary system.

Assessing Quality in Postsecondary Education: International Perspectives, edited by Harvey P. Weingarten, Martin Hicks, and Amy Kaufman. Montréal and Kingston: McGill-Queen's University Press, Queen's Policy Studies Series. © 2018 The School of Policy Studies, Queen's University at Kingston. All rights reserved.

traditional 18–23 age group (HEA 2016b). Fewer than 10 percent of students are international, although the aim is to increase that figure to 15 percent by 2020 (DES 2016a). Over the last decades, participation rates have risen rapidly to a point where Ireland is now anticipating rates of over 60 percent, which place it at the upper end of benchmarking levels for the EU and the Organisation for Economic Co-operation and Development (OECD).

The Great Recession, which followed the global financial crisis and the banking collapse in 2008, had a profound impact on Ireland (Whelan 2013). Funding levels for higher education collapsed at the same time that student demand increased, resulting in a significant decline in funding per student, dropping from about €12,000 per student in 2008 to a little over €9,000 by 2015 (Expert Group on Future Funding for Higher Education 2016, 67). At the same time, unemployment rose from a low of about 4 percent in 2008 to over 12 percent by 2012, with graduate unemployment rising to 6 percent (CSO 2017). The latter would likely have been higher were it not for significant increases in emigration (CSO 2016; Riegel 2013). Almost ten years on, Ireland is now looking at projections of sustained economic growth and increasing demand for higher education, driven by that growth as well as by demographics (McQuinn, Foley, and O'Toole 2017). Ireland has the highest birth rate among EU countries and the lowest death rate (Power 2017). Current projections estimate that the size of the higher-education system will increase by more than 20 percent over the coming fifteen years (DES 2015). A key factor in Ireland's economic development during the past decades has been policies that have favoured internationally traded services and foreign direct investment, and that have strengthened Ireland's position as a knowledge-based society (Whittaker 1958); this has put human capital at the forefront. Accordingly, questions are regularly focused on the quality of graduates and graduate attributes (Clancy 2015; McGuinness, O'Shaughnessy, and Pouliakas 2017). The combination of these issues has encouraged greater political scrutiny of Ireland's higher-education system and calls for greater forms of accountability.

This chapter reviews the current measures being taken to assess teaching and learning and student satisfaction, and what role these measures play in setting higher-education policy and resource allocation. It will also consider efforts being taken to improve understanding and reporting on the nature of the student experience, and the quality of teaching and learning within Irish higher education. The system is currently undergoing considerable change. While there are no definitive findings as yet, indications of future directions are emerging.

Historical Context

The 1960s are commonly seen as a turning point in the development of Irish higher education and, correspondingly, the transformation of the Irish economy from a rural inwardly facing society to a post-industrial openly trading one. Indeed, there is an inextricable link between these two factors (Barry 2007). Prior to that, the system was small, in terms of both the number of institutions and students attending, and was not seen as a significant element of wider national development. Participation levels were around 10 percent, and entry was strongly related to ability to pay not only tuition costs at the tertiary or higher education level, but also costs at the secondary level given that it was not free at that time.

Two very significant developments changed this picture during the 1960s (White 2001). First, the government instigated the Commission on Higher Education in 1960 (DES 1967), with a mandate to consider how higher education could support wider national development, particularly economic development (Coolahan 1990). Second, the government made secondary education free to all students in 1968, which further contributed to the trend of growing participation, and, correspondingly, increased demand for places in higher education.

The findings of the commission contributed to a greater awareness of the role of higher education in providing the requisite skills for Ireland's continued economic development, and, following further follow-up reviews, led to the creation of a new sector of Irish higher education, the regional technical colleges (O'Connor 2014). This sector was created with a very explicit mandate to provide students with a vocationally oriented education that would meet the needs of a growing industrial sector, both indigenous and foreign. The government also created two additional institutions—known as the National Institute of Higher Education, Dublin and the National Institute of Higher Education, Limerick, both of which also had an orientation toward meeting growing economic demand for skilled graduates. In addition, the government established a separate statutory agency, the Higher Education Authority (HEA), to manage the allocation of funding for higher education and provide policy advice on the further development of the sector (GoI 1971).

These developments led to a steady increase in participation rates in higher education. By 1980 those levels had reached 20 percent (Clancy 2015, 36) and would steadily increase over the coming decades to reach the current level of about 60 percent (HEA 2015b). In parallel with the growing levels of participation, the HEA instigated a regular review process of entry to the system, undertaking a study every six years on access to higher education, which measured participation by the socio-economic origin of students. These studies showed marked disparities between higher and lower socio-economic groupings; these divergences have begun to diminish as participation among those from higher socio-economic groups reached saturation levels (i.e., virtually all students in those groups were progressing to higher education) and as general participation levels continued to rise (Clancy 2015, 66–72; O'Connell, McCoy, and Clancy 2006).

The rapid transformation of the higher-education system from the 1960s onward was mainly focused on undergraduate education and teaching. Very little funding or focus was paid to the development of research capacity and performance in higher education, so much so that in 1996 an HEA study found very little research activity across the system (CIRCA Group 1996). The chief funders were private entities (such as medical charities) and some funding was provided by the EU. That began to change in 1998, principally through major new funding schemes run by the HEA (mainly through the Programme for Research in Third Level Institutions and philanthropic funding from the Atlantic Philanthropies), and subsequently by the establishment of a new research funding agency, the Science Foundation Ireland (SFI), as well as research funding councils supporting early-career researchers across all disciplines. SFI was positioned as part of an industrial strategy, with the specific mandate to invest research funding in priority areas that would encourage Ireland's economic development—a new model based on knowledge rather than cost advantages (DETE 2006).

By 2006, the Irish system had made very rapid progress and was performing well in providing mass higher education. There was also good evidence that investment in research was rapidly building capacity in the system, and that areas of very high research performance were beginning to emerge. Indeed, by 2012, Ireland was identified by *Nature* as a "country to watch" buoyed by a "science-friendly regime" (Swinbanks 2012, 1, 25–26). The National Research Prioritisation Exercise, conducted in the wake of the Great Recession, controversially tied research funding to designated economic sectors, although it enabled ongoing funding at a time when core teaching and learning funding was declining (Research Prioritisation Steering Group 2011).

In terms of assessing teaching quality and the student experience, the system has developed a number of initiatives, of which the last two are indirect or proxy measures of teaching quality. These include:

- Building a retention factor into the funding model—Institutions are funded on the basis of student numbers, weighted by academic discipline. Student numbers are counted only in March. As a result, institutions that see students dropping out by that date are not funded for those students. This has created a strong financial incentive for institutions to support students in continuing their studies.
- Creation of a quality assurance system—This has involved subject, faculty, and institutional reviews with national and international peers, from the academic, employer, and student sectors.
- Surveys of graduates—These are conducted by the HEA and by individual higher-education institutions to assess the position of graduates post-graduation (e.g., employment, further education, or unemployed), as well as their salary levels.
- Surveys of employers—The National Employer Survey is commissioned by the HEA in partnership with SOLAS, the Further Education and Training Authority, and Quality and Qualifications Ireland. The survey collects the views of employers on education outcomes.

In 2013, the system took another significant step forward with the creation of what is known as the "strategic dialogue" process (HEA 2017a). The *National Strategy for Higher Education to 2030* proposed the creation of service-level agreements. The objective was to improve institutional performance through the development of a more formal process of establishing goals and associated metrics of performance, and to hold institutions to account by referencing aggregated institutional performance against national overarching performance goals. In addition, strategic dialogue would "enable consideration of the sum of the institutional plans to test for overall system coherence and completeness, to ensure national needs are being met, and to identify and address unnecessary duplication" (Strategy Group 2011, 92).

Strategic Dialogue Process

The framework for the dialogue process is set out in Figure 5.1. There are three distinct steps: (1) the government sets high-level objectives for the system to deliver over a defined period; (2) institutions prepare their own plans, taking into account their particular mission, regional needs, and institutional ambitions, and ensuring that they align with the national objectives; and (3) the HEA meets each institution and reaches a compact that sets the basis for assessing institutional performance, and delivering the wider national objectives of the government.

The national framework, prepared for the first time by the minister in 2013, set out an agenda for the following three-year period. It referenced seven major domains against which system performance would be assessed (DES 2013, 2).

1. To meet Ireland's human-capital needs across the spectrum of skills by engaged institutions through a diverse mix of provision across the system and through both core funding and specifically targeted initiatives

2. To promote access for disadvantaged groups and put in place coherent pathways from second-level education, further education, and other non-traditional entry routes

3. To promote excellence in teaching and learning to underpin a high-quality student experience

4. To maintain an open and excellent public-research system focused on the government's priority areas and the achievement of other societal objectives, and to maximize research collaborations and knowledge exchange between and among public- and private-sector research actors

5. To ensure that Ireland's higher-education institutions will be globally competitive and internationally oriented, and that Ireland will be a world-class centre of international education

6. To reform practices and restructure the system for quality and diversity

7. To increase accountability of autonomous institutions for public funding and against national priorities

In the case of Objective 3—teaching and learning and the student experience—the system framework referenced the following metrics of

Figure 5.1

Strategic Dialogue and the Development of Metrics Around Teaching and Quality of the Student Experience

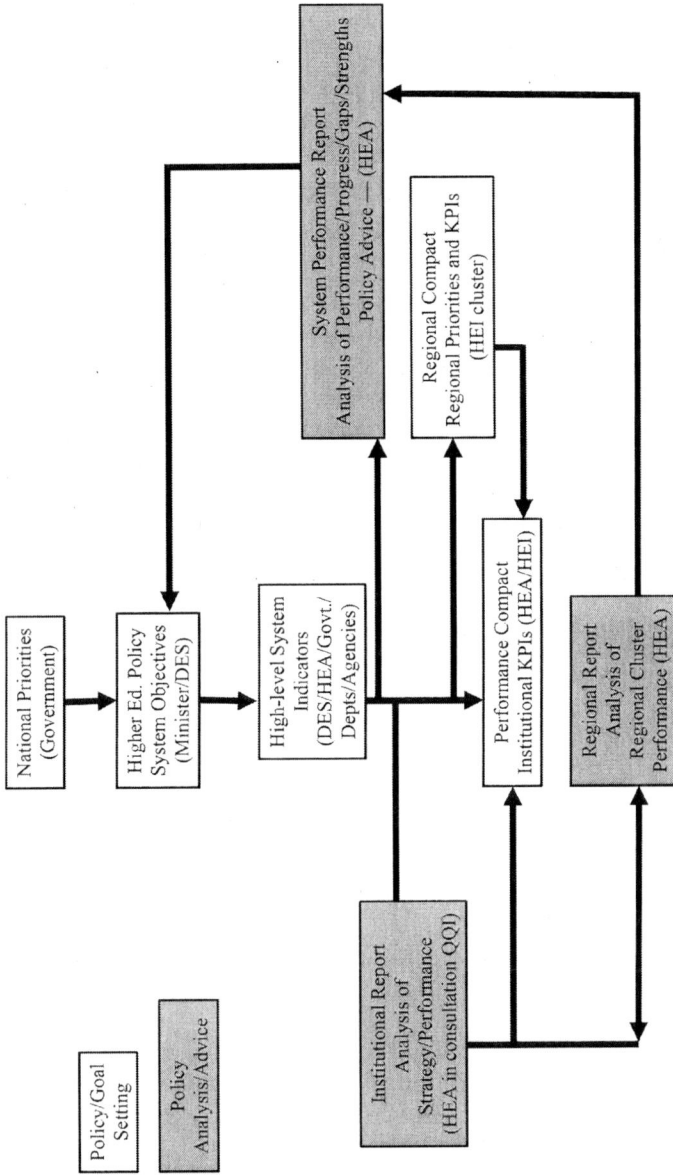

Policy/Goal Setting

Policy Analysis/Advice

National Priorities (Government)

Higher Ed. Policy System Objectives (Minister/DES)

High-level System Indicators (DES/HEA/Govt./Depts/Agencies)

System Performance Report Analysis of Performance/Progress/Gaps/Strengths Policy Advice — (HEA)

Regional Compact Regional Priorities and KPIs (HEI cluster)

Performance Compact Institutional KPIs (HEA/HEI)

Institutional Report Analysis of Strategy/Performance (HEA in consultation QQI)

Regional Report Analysis of Regional Cluster Performance (HEA)

Source: DES (2013, 3)

performance:

- Quality assurance—all higher-education institutions would undertake quality-assurance procedures in line with European best practices
- Student engagement and satisfaction scores—institutional scores in the National Student Survey would be monitored
- Progression rates from first to second year would be measured at an institutional disciplinary and program level
- Proliferation of entry points into higher education would be reduced—this arose from a concern that students entering higher education were facing difficulties stemming from higher-education institutions creating large numbers of very specific programs as a means to boost enrolment, but which created unnecessary confusion among students
- Finally, the ratio of students to teaching staff in educational institutions would be assessed, relative to EU and OECD averages

These metrics illustrate some of the difficulties associated with the framework, as they combine fairly routine processes (like quality assurance), with very specific and focused indicators (like reducing program numbers) along with fairly routine data that HEA would have produced in any case (non-progression and student-to-staff ratios; see discussion below).

The framework also provided what were called essential indicators, which were not meant to be metrics in themselves, but would be activities considered essential to deliver the metrics. Importantly, these included a requirement to monitor how institutions themselves were embedding a focus on excellence in teaching and learning within institutional strategies. This was an enabling measure; it provided scope for the HEA to engage with the institutions in more detail and to understand what actions were being taken locally. In doing so, this reinforced an overall objective of the framework, which was to enhance diversity among institutions within the system.

Finally, in addition to the creation of the new framework, further enabling measures were introduced to assist in understanding the quality of teaching and the student experience. Perhaps the most important of these was the creation of an Irish Survey of Student Engagement (ISSE),[2] which initially closely matched the Australasian Survey of Stu-

---

2   The Irish Survey of Student Engagement is managed as a collaborative partnership.

dent Engagement (AUSSE), and more recently the US National Survey of Student Engagement (NSSE). The national-level findings of the Irish survey are published, while institutional findings are only available privately so that institutions can understand their performance.

The role of the HEA is to reach compacts with each institution. Each institution is asked to submit its own performance goals and associated indicators of improvement as part of a three-year compact with the HEA. Failure to deliver on the compact leaves the institution vulnerable to a reduction in state funding. There are, however, no set metrics that an institution is required to follow; instead, the HEA has stressed that institutions need to develop and defend their own assessment frameworks by providing robust data to set a baseline against which future improvement will be measured. The HEA has reserved the right to reject compacts proposed by institutions where, for example, the objectives are of poor quality or lack sufficient or inappropriate ambition.

In their responses, higher-education institutions have shown considerable diversity in their compacts. In terms of the quality of teaching, they returned a range of goals with respect to the following areas:

- Academic staff development
- Enhanced quality-assurance processes
- Student induction or initiation events
- Student retention rates
- Online programs and student enrolment,
- Graduate attributes and implementing them in all programs
- Measuring and improving employability
- Curriculum reform (opportunities to take a wide selection of disciplines at the undergraduate level)
- Student satisfaction (using the Irish Survey of Student Engagement)
- Student engagement in community-based learning
- Integration of research into undergraduate learning

The HEA set the compacts in 2014, and reviewed performance annually in 2015, 2016, and 2017. In general, institutions have made good progress against the goals they set, but to what extent this is improving their strategic capacity or the quality and assessment of teaching and

---

It is co-sponsored by the Higher Education Authority, institutions' representative bodies (the Irish Universities Association, and the Technological Higher Education Association) and the Union of Students in Ireland.

learning is less certain. The Irish government is currently preparing the next national performance framework.

Assessing Progress and Looking Ahead

As discussed above, the idea of establishing a framework for a new social contract between Ireland's higher-education institutions and society was strongly recommended in the *National Strategy for Higher Education to 2030*. It referred to the desire to establish "a new contractual relationship or service level agreement...as part of a wider strategic dialogue, and this should be used to ensure that the requirements for performance, autonomy and accountability are aligned" (Strategy Group 2011, 14).

The completion of the first full round of strategic dialogue in 2017, involving three annual meetings plus numerous pre- and post-dialogue meetings, presents a good opportunity to reflect, assess, and look forward. A few issues of context first.

The strategic dialogue process was predicated on the necessity for (better) alignment between higher education, its objectives and outcomes, and Irish national objectives; or to use a broader concept, "the public good" (Hazelkorn and Gibson 2017). While there has been a strong social justice and equity component to Irish education policy making since the founding of the state in 1922 (Hazelkorn, Gibson, and Harkin 2015), formally embedding national objectives as a strategic purpose into higher-education policy marked a radical departure. The institutes of technology, originally called Regional Technical Colleges (RTC), were established between 1967 and 2000, with the defined mandate to underpin industrial development following the recommendations of the Steering Committee on Technical Education in 1967 (GoI 1967; Walsh 2009). In contrast, the universities have traditionally had a broader mandate, although since the Universities Act of 1997, they have had a legislative requirement "to support and contribute to the realization of the national and social development" (Universities Act 1997). Nonetheless, the strategic dialogue process represented a point at which the government formally articulated "the public good" and higher-education institutions were asked through a series of institutional submissions, discussions, and negotiations to affirm the extent to which they could meet those objectives. Accordingly, a dialogue between the institutions and the HEA, on behalf of the government, ensued.

For both parties, strategic dialogue signalled other profound changes that stemmed from this greater focus on strategic direction and measuring outcomes. The National Strategy put the HEA front and centre in leading the "creation of a co-ordinated system of higher-education institutions with clear and diverse roles appropriate to their strengths and national needs." (HEA 2017b). In turn, the government introduced national performance targets marked by a service-level agreement with the HEA (DES 2016b). Thus, strategic dialogue marked a point where the government, through the HEA, for the first time had to state clearly its policy objectives and what it wanted from higher education. In return, the IoTs and the universities had to clearly articulate their own visions, missions, objectives, and targets in a format open to scrutiny by the HEA and an international panel. Moreover, institutional submissions were publicly available on the HEA website, and thus accessible to examination and analysis by peer institutions, politicians, the public, and researchers. Certainly, the universities had more experience and capacity for this type of endeavour than the IoTs, but it's been a learning curve for all concerned. The IoTs had historically been closely monitored by the Department of Education, with decisions, course proposals, and scrutinized budgets—the latter often on a line-by-line basis. While this changed in 2006 when authority for the IoTs transferred to the HEA, they have for myriad reasons been slow to develop sufficient strategic capacity and capability. Institutional research competence is uneven across institutions. Even the HEA, with a statutory responsibility for effective governance and regulation of the higher-education system, has had to learn new skills.

There have been other challenges associated with the overall purpose of the exercise, *inter alia* identifying mission-oriented objectives, setting realistic and realizable targets, and then being able to communicate this information to government and the public.

There are probably three broad approaches to performance assessment:

- Performance via greater transparency, using greater levels of reporting on what is being delivered by higher education, such as graduate outcomes, student feedback, quality reviews, etc.
- Performance via funding, using particular targets to widen access or reduce dropout rates, etc.
- Performance assessment via compacts, using a set of guidelines and a process of negotiated agreements or compacts (de Boer et al. 2015, 2; Benneworth et al. 2011)

Arguably, Ireland has adopted all three approaches, which has effectively meant evolving over time from remote to more direct steerage in response to the changed economic and political climate. Today, Ireland's focus is on the third category, without fully abandoning concepts of the previous arrangement. This has involved the HEA preparing a guiding template, indicating broad expectations of all institutions, regardless of scale, sector, or mission. It was centred on the ability of the institution to set and meet goals in its own institutional context, with the aim of strengthening the long-term strategic capacity and capability of institutions. Effectively, this is an instrument that seeks to balance institutional autonomy with social accountability as a new form of social contract.

There are inevitable tensions, however. For example, the government has identified the overarching objectives for the sector, but the framework as a whole could be said to be incomplete. It does not address critical, perhaps essential, questions, the most obvious of which is how large the system should be, and what sort of funding model would support such a system. While these issues are shaped by the HEA funding model, which requires institutions to grow at least at the rate of the sector average in order to avoid losing their share of funding, key questions about the size, shape, and direction of the system remain within the purview of institutions.[3]

Institutional progress is monitored according to:

- How well an institution understands itself, its mission and its goals
- How well it has set out its ambitions for improvement
- How it measures its success in that regard
- How it learns as it changes

However, the choice of targets and indicators raises another set of challenges. As noted above, the HEA did not set specific targets or metrics, but expected each institution to prioritize a particular set of activities. Ultimately, each institution was required to satisfactorily explain how it was addressing these challenges, and demonstrate that policies appropriate to its institutional mission and context were in place.

---

3 The Irish higher-education model does not cap numbers nor does it link the size of the funding allocation to the numbers of students. However, all funds come from the same pot. Thus, institutions grow their share of state funding by growing student numbers, thus forcing other institutions to match the overall system growth rate. The overall effect is to reduce the overall funding per student.

In reviewing the initial results of the process, it is quite evident that it has not created a simple system by which to assess how each institution is itself assessing the quality of teaching and the student experience, nor has it created a system of easy comparison. There are myriad indicators, as well as institutional approaches, levels of ambition, and capacity and capability to deliver. While this exemplifies a diverse system, it makes the task of communicating how well our institutions are delivering higher quality teaching more difficult than before. There is so much to communicate, and much of it is qualitative and at a fairly granular level. It is true that the HEA may be much better informed than previously, and better able to understand the position of the various institutions, but for the HEA merely to report that this is the outcome is not particularly useful for government or other stakeholders. At this stage, the process itself is still considered important, and it is hoped that it offers the potential to further expand and develop. The following issues are worth noting.

First, it is an underpinning principle that institutions themselves should develop a medium-term strategic perspective on what they wish to achieve and the pathway to achieving it. In doing so, this forces institutions to consider questions such as:

- How do we currently measure quality?
- How do we estimate how we are doing relative to peers or benchmark institutions?
- How can we address weak points or build on strong areas?
- How is this integrated with wider institutional objectives, like internationalization, research performance, or broadening access?

While some institutions are well advanced in managing such discussions at an institutional level, it is also clear that for many this is a new process. The reality is that all institutions were not starting from the same place. This was partially evidenced by the fact that IoTs performed least well in an informal "ranking," lending credence to the notion that the system was not just differentiated but also stratified. The process also relies heavily on the capacity of the HEA and its international team to examine the documents and institutional statements.

Second, while there is a diversity of responses as to how institutions responded to this challenge, there are also similarities. A majority of institutes cited goals or targets in the following areas:

- Academic staff development
- Enhancement of quality-assurance processes

- Student induction or initiation
- Student retention rates
- Student satisfaction
- Measurement and improvement of employability

Not surprisingly, these are essential areas for each institution to be able to demonstrate to external audiences. However, this doesn't mean that the institutions should be alike in how they tackle the issues; in fact, it is desirable that they should be different and recognize their different missions, as well as their different starting points. In addition, there should be a further layer of objectives that are more specific to each institution. In the current round of compacts these include:

- Broad curriculum opportunities
- Student engagement in community-based learning
- Integration of research into undergraduate learning
- Development of graduate attributes and implementation in all programs
- Increased online programs and student enrolment

These differences were not always as apparent as might have been anticipated, indicating the extent to which there is a general convergence in educational practices.

Third, there is some evidence that institutions are being encouraged (forced?) to reassess their priorities. In a roundabout way, student experience may be a beneficiary of this process. For example, when the compacts were initially set, there was a deliberate attempt by institutions to use the compacts and associated goals to mark out territory in which they wished to be involved. Many smaller institutions provided quite ambitious targets with respect to research (e.g., number of research students, competitive income earned, etc.) Over the years, some institutions have sought to downgrade research targets, reflecting their lack of capacity as well as overly ambitious goals. At the same time, these institutions began to enhance their activity around the student experience, most notably student retention. Driven perhaps by increasing data around student performance and, correspondingly, easy inter-institutional comparisons, the institutions began to identify areas where they could avoid being seen as poor performers. Relatedly, there is also evidence of inter-institutional learning of good practices. This is most evident with respect to retention, with different institutions demonstrating and sharing techniques to address high dropout rates, and incorporating this into their own processes and goal setting. These actions suggest encouraging aspects of how the process, by bringing greater transparency to institutional performance, can assist in improving performance both within and between institutions, although it is still early days.

Finally, the ·strategic dialogue process sought to focus attention around a key set of priorities. Hitherto, the system has been laden with multiple objectives and stakeholders, that to identify and prioritize a particular set was confusing and led to a diminution of regard for some that remained implicit, and/or an actual deterioration of performance for others, such as retention and access. The multiplicity of objectives is best illustrated by an exercise conducted by the HEA that identified a bewildering array of almost 100 different targets written into various national reviews or policy statements from across government. It is probably inevitable that each review will produce a report with recommendations and indications. But the aggregate of these processes reflects an international predilection for "governmental knowledge through quantification," which can easily lead to unintended incentives and consequences (Rottenburg et al. 2015). On the other hand, picking a handful of indicators carries other difficulties associated with driving homogeneity. To date, the only common metrics in the system are student numbers by program type, which are used as the fundamental unit for funding the system.

At the same time, there remains confusion around terminology. For example, engagement is a national objective, but what it means and measures varies considerably: is it primarily technology transfer or does it involve a more holistic engagement with local/civil society (Hazelkorn 2016)? Attention to the quality, value, or sustainability of the initiatives has been lost in the overall process of measuring. Ultimately, for a small system, looking at each institution in terms of its own mission and targets can obscure wider questions about overall system performance and direction, including issues of efficiency, effectiveness, and competitiveness.

These latter points highlight another challenge as public entities everywhere are under pressure to be more accountable. Thus, how the HEA and institutions individually and collectively communicate higher education's contribution, value, and benefit to society and the economy remains problematic. The problem afflicts both the choice of indicators and the format. The current compacts are quite fragmented, too detailed to be accessible to anyone but the most interested reader, and difficult to use as a benchmarking instrument. The HEA published a substantial report following each process (HEA 2015a; 2016a), and it has also published institutional and sector profiles that aim to highlight institutional differentiation (HEA 2015c; 2016c). Yet, it's unclear the extent to which these reports are read by the political or public community. Indeed, the emergence and fascination with rankings is partly attributable to the availability of easily understood and readable comparable information and data that can inform student choice or decision making by governments or institutions (Hazelkorn 2015).

The role and ability of the HEA to govern the system is also coming under scrutiny. As mentioned above, the HEA has had to strengthen its own data collection and analysis capacity, as well as its ability to interrogate institutional activity and progress. More recently, there has been growing political pressure on the HEA to show that it is exercising its governance authority for the system as a whole, assuring value-for-money, and, correspondingly, enhancing its regulatory functions. This has most recently emerged in the context of a controversy concerning the use (or misuse) of public funds by some higher-education institutions (O'Brien 2017) and discussions within the parliamentary Public Accounts Committee. There are implications for the organization and its priorities.

In January 2018, the government launched the 2018–2020 Performance Framework, setting out key objectives for the higher-education system (DES 2018). As the HEA reviews the strategic dialogue processes, what lessons can be learned? What needs to change to keep the process fresh and meaningful? Is there scope for a broader mandate for HEA interactions with the institutions? To what extent should a balance be struck between common and institutional customized indicators, and how should this be done? Should access to particular funding schemes, or permission to depart from national frameworks be dependent upon performance? How much and what type of information is required and by whom? For example, would a two-tier system of indicators and reporting—one for the institutions and one for the public, with government choosing to use either or both—be more useful? And ultimately, what is the role and purpose of the strategic dialogue, how effective has it been and how effective can it be in improving the quality of educational outcomes and in shaping a common perspective on the role and contribution of Irish higher education? These and other questions are all up for consideration as Ireland enters the next phase of the strategic dialogue process.

References

Barry, Frank. 2007. "Third-level Education, Foreign Direct Investment and Economic Boom in Ireland." *International Journal of Technology Management* 38 (3): 198–219.

Benneworth, Paul S., Harry F. de Boer, Leon Cremonini, Benjamin W. A. Jongbloed, Liudvika Leisyte, Johan J. Vossensteyn, and Egbert de Weert. 2011. *Quality-Related Funding, Performance Agreements and Profiling in Higher Education: An International Comparative Study.* Enschede: Centre for Higher Education Policy Studies (CHEPS).

CIRCA Group. 1996. *A Comparative International Assessment of the Organisation, Management and Funding of University Research in Ireland and Europe.* Dublin: HEA.

Clancy, Patrick. 2015. *Irish Higher Education: A Comparative Perspective.* Dublin: Institute of Public Administration.

Coolahan, John. 1990. "The Commission on Higher Education, 1967, and Third-Level Policy in Contemporary Ireland." *Irish Educational Studies* 9 (1): 1–12. https://doi.org/10.1080/0332331900090104

CSO (Central Statistics Office). 2016. *Population and Emigration Estimates.* Dublin: Central Statistics Office. http://www.cso.ie/en/releasesandpublications/er/pme/populationandmigrationestimatesapril2016/;

———. 2017. *Census 2016 Summary Results—Part 2.* Dublin: Central Statistics Office. http://www.cso.ie/en/media/csoie/newsevents/documents/census2016summaryresultspart2/Census_2016_Summary_Results_-_Part_2_-_Launch_Presentation_FINAL.pdf

de Boer, Harry F., Benjamin W. A. Jongbloed, Paul S. Benneworth, Leon Cremonini, Renze Kolster, Andrea Kottmann, Katharina Lemmens-Krug, and Johan J. Vossensteyn. 2015. *Performance-Based Funding and Performance Agreements in Fourteen Higher Education Systems.* Enschede: Centre for Higher Education Policy Studies (CHEPS).

DES (Department of Education and Skills). 1967. *Report of the Commission on Higher Education.* Dublin: Department of Education.

———. 2013. *Higher Education System Performance Framework, 2014–2016.* Dublin: Department of Education and Skills. http://hea.ie/assets/uploads/2017/06/DES-System-Performance-Framework.pdf

———. 2015. *Projections of Demand for Full Time Third Level Education, 2015–2029.* Dublin: Department of Education and Skills. https://www.education.ie/en/Publications/Statistics/Statistical-Reports/Projections-of-demand-for-full-time-Third-Level-Education-2015-2029.pdf

———. 2016a. *Irish Educated Globally Connected: An International Edu-*

cation Strategy for Ireland, 2016–2020. Dublin: Department of Education and Skills. https://www.education.ie/en/Publications/Policy-Reports/International-Education-Strategy-For-Ireland-2016-2020.pdf

———. 2016b. *Service Level Agreement: Department of Education and Skills and Higher Education Authority*. Dublin: Department of Education and Skills. http://hea.ie/assets/uploads/2017/04/Service-level-Agreement-2016.pdf

———. 2018. Higher Education System Performance Framework 2018–2020. Dublin: Department of Education and Skills. http://www.hea.ie/2018/01/15/hea-welcomes-publication-of-funding-allocation-model-review-and-revised-system-performance-framework/

DETE (Department of Enterprise, Trade, and Employment). 2006. *Strategy for Science, Technology and Innovation 2006–2013*. Dublin: Department of Enterprise, Trade and Employment. https://www.djei.ie/en/Publications/Publication-files/Forfás/Strategy-for-Science-Technology-and-Innovation-2006-2013.pdf

Expert Group on Future Funding for Higher Education. 2016. *Investing in National Ambition: A Strategy for Funding Higher Education*. Dublin. https://www.education.ie/en/Publications/Policy-Reports/Investing-in-National-Ambition-A-Strategy-for-Funding-Higher-Education.pdf

GoI (Government of Ireland). 1967. *Steering Committee on Technical Education: Report to the Minister for Education on Regional Technical Colleges*. Dublin: Government of Ireland.

———. 1971. *Higher Education Authority Act, 1971*. Dublin: Irish Statute Books. http://www.irishstatutebook.ie/eli/1971/act/22/enacted/en/html

Hazelkorn, Ellen. 2015. *Rankings and the Reshaping of Higher Education: The Battle for World-Class Excellence*, 2nd ed. Palgrave Macmillan UK.

———. 2016. "Contemporary Debates Part 1: Theorising Civic Engagement." In *The Civic University: The Policy and Leadership Challenges*, edited by John Goddard, Ellen Hazelkorn, Louise Kempton and Paul Vallance, 34–64. Cheltenham: Edward Elgar.

Hazelkorn, Ellen, and Andrew Gibson. 2017. *Public Goods and Public Policy: What Is Public Good, and Who and What Decides?* Centre for Global Higher Education Working Paper No. 18. http://www.researchcghe.org/perch/resources/publications/wp18.pdf

Hazelkorn, Ellen, Andrew Gibson, and Siobhán Harkin. 2015. "Irish Higher Education from Massification to Globalisation: Reflections on the Transformation of Irish Higher Education." In *The State in Transition: Essays in Honour of John Horgan*, edited by Kevin Rafter and Mark O'Brien, 235–60. Dublin: O'Brien Press.

HEA (Higher Education Authority). 2015a. *Higher Education System Performance, First Report 2014–2016*. Report of the Higher Education Authority to the Minister for Education and Skills. Dublin: Higher Education Authority. https://www.education.ie/en/Publications/Education-Reports/Higher-Education-System-Performance-First-report-2014-2016.pdf

———. 2015b. *National Plan for Equity of Access to Higher Education 2015–2019*. Dublin: Higher Education Authority.

———. 2015c. *Higher Education System Performance. First Report 2014–2016 Volume II. Institutional and Sectoral Profiles 2011–12.* Report of the Higher Education Authority. Dublin: Higher Education Authority. http://hea.ie/assets/uploads/2017/06/Institutional-Profiles-2011-12.pdf

———. 2016a. *Higher Education System Performance, 2014–2016*. Second Report of the Higher Education Authority to the Minister for Education and Skills. Dublin: Higher Education Authority. http://hea.ie/assets/uploads/2017/06/Higher-Education-System-Performance-2014–2016.pdf

———. 2016b. *Key Facts and Figures*. Dublin: Higher Education Authority. http://hea.ie/assets/uploads/2017/06/HEA-Key-Facts-and-Figures-201516.pdf

———. 2016c. *Higher Education System Performance Institutional and Sectoral Profiles 2013/14*. A Report by the Higher Education Authority. Dublin: Higher Education Authority. http://hea.ie/assets/uploads/2016/11/Higher-Education-System-Performance-Institutional-and-Sectoral-Profiles-201314.pdf

———. 2017a. "Strategic Dialogue." Higher Education Authority. http://hea.ie/funding-governance-performance/managing-performance/strategic-dialogue/

———. 2017b. "About Us: Overview." Higher Education Authority. http://hea.ie/about-us/overview/

McGuinness, Seamus, Ruth O'Shaughnessy, and Konstantinos Pouliakas. 2017. "Overeducation in the Irish Labour Market." In *Economic Insights on Higher Education Policy in Ireland. Evidence from a Public System*, edited by John Cullinan and Darragh Flannery, 165–96. Basingstoke: Palgrave MacMillan.

McQuinn, Kieran, Daniel Foley, and Conor O'Toole. 2017. *Quarterly Economic Commentary: Summer 2017*. Dublin: Economic and Social Research Institute (ESRI). https://www.esri.ie/pubs/QEC2017SUM_2.pdf

O'Brien, Carl. 2017. "Universities Face Severe Criticism over Use of Public Funds." *The Irish Times*, 11 July. https://www.irishtimes.com/

news/education/universities-face-severe-criticism-over-use-of-public-funds-1.3150051

O'Connell, Philip J., Selina McCoy, and David Clancy. 2006. "Who Went to College? Socio-Economic Inequality in Entry to Higher Education in the Republic of Ireland in 2004." *Higher Education Quarterly* 60 (4): 312–332. https://doi.org/10.1111/j.1468-2273.2006.00326.x

O'Connor, Muiris. 2014. "Investment in Edification: Reflections on Irish Education Policy Since Independence." *Irish Educational Studies* 33 (2): 193–212. https://doi.org/10.1080/03323315.2014.920609

Power, Jack. 2017. "Baby Boom Puts Ireland Top of EU Birth Rate Table." *The Irish Times*. 10 July. https://www.irishtimes.com/news/ireland/irish-news/baby-boom-puts-ireland-top-of-eu-birth-rate-table-1.3150045

Research Prioritisation Steering Group. 2011. *Report of the Research Prioritisation Steering Group*. Dublin: Department of Jobs, Enterprise and Innovation. https://dbei.gov.ie/en/Publications/Publication-files/Research-Prioritisation.pdf

Riegel, Ralph. 2013. "Highly Qualified Graduates Now Make Up Majority of Emigrants." *Irish Independent*. 27 September. http://www.independent.ie/life/family/learning/highly-qualified-graduates-now-make-up-majority-of-emigrants-29614325.html

Rottenburg, Richard, Sally E. Merry, Sung-Joon Park, and Johanna Mugler, eds. 2015. *The World of Indicators: The Making of Governmental Knowledge through Quantification*. Cambridge: Cambridge University Press.

Strategy Group. 2011. *National Strategy for Higher Education to 2030*. Dublin: Department of Education and Skills. http://hea.ie/assets/uploads/2017/06/National-Strategy-for-Higher-Education-2030.pdf

Swinbanks, David. 2012 "Five Countries to Watch." *Nature Publishing Index 2012* 25–26. https://www.natureasia.com/en/publishing-index/pdf/NPI2012_Global.pdf

Universities Act. 1997. Dublin: Irish Statute Book. http://www.irishstatutebook.ie/eli/1997/act/24/section/12/enacted/en/html#sec12

Walsh, John. 2009. *The Politics of Expansion: The Transformation of Educational Policy in the Republic of Ireland, 1957–72*. Manchester: Manchester University Press.

———. 2014a. "The Transformation of Higher Education in Ireland, 1945–80." In *Higher Education in Ireland: Practices, Policies and Possibilities*, edited by Andrew Loxley, Aidan Seery, and John Walsh, 5–32. Basingstoke: Palgrave MacMillan.

———. 2014b. "A Contemporary History of Irish Higher Education,"

In *Higher Education in Ireland: Practices, Policies and Possibilities,* edited by Andrew Loxley, Aidan Seery, and John Walsh 33–54. Basingstoke: Palgrave MacMillan.

Whelan, Karl. 2013. "Ireland's Economic Crisis. The Good, the Bad and the Ugly." Paper presented at Bank of Greece Conference on the Euro Crisis, Athens, 24 May. http://www.karlwhelan.com/Papers/Whelan-IrelandPaper-June2013.pdf

White, Tony. 2001. *Investing in People. Higher Education in Ireland from 1960–2000.* Dublin: Institute of Public Administration.

Whittaker, Thomas Kenneth. 1958. *Economic Development.* Dublin: Department of Finance/Stationery Office.

6

Performance Contracts: A New Tool in Higher-Education Governance

Frans van Vught

Higher-Education Governance

Governance of and in higher-education systems is a topic with its own historical roots and models. For a long time continental European governments, with all the existing variations, have been the prime funders and the overarching and powerful regulators of their higher-education systems. According to the so-called "state-control model" of governance, the government controls, at least formally, nearly all aspects of the dynamics of the higher-education system. It regulates institutional missions, access, curricula, degrees, academic staff appointments, and labour conditions. It owns buildings, property, and physical assets, and it prescribes in detail how public funds are to be spent (line-item budgeting).

An alternative governance model, called the "state-supervisory model," has its roots both in the US and the traditional British higher-education systems. The American and British models show far less governmental influence on higher education than the continental model. The government sees itself as a supervisor, steering from a distance and using broad terms of regulation, stimulating the self-regulating capabilities of the higher-education institutions (Clark 1983, 127).

In recent decades, several governance reforms have taken place.

Assessing Quality in Postsecondary Education: International Perspectives, edited by Harvey P. Weingarten, Martin Hicks, and Amy Kaufman. Montréal and Kingston: McGill-Queen's University Press, Queen's Policy Studies Series. © 2018 The School of Policy Studies, Queen's University at Kingston. All rights reserved.

These transformations worked out differently for the traditional modes of governance. In general, the traditional British state-supervising model has moved somewhat toward a "non-British" state-control model, whereas in many continental systems a clear shift from state control to state supervision has become visible (van Vught 1989; Neave and van Vught 1991; de Boer et al. 2010). In the US, the government's authority in general has been growing, but this increase has moved toward "adaptations of market control mechanisms" such as outcomes-assessment legislation and performance-based funding (Dill 1992, 53–4).

Generally speaking, most governments nowadays acknowledge that local diversities exist on the part of higher-education institutions. They realize that these institutions will have to have regard for the needs of their own stakeholders and local clienteles. Thus, governments have adapted their governance approaches accordingly, allowing higher-education institutions substantial autonomy, and offering them sufficient opportunities to refine and adapt national policies to reflect local differences. Some governments seek to empower students and external stakeholders to exert more influence over higher-education institutions, while others refrain from detailed top-down regulation. Yet other authorities look for "smart" governance approaches that combine vertical steering (traditional public administration) with elements of market-type mechanisms (new public management).

However, during the last few years, a new critique has emerged regarding this supervisory governance model. Two major points of criticism appear to be dominant. First, doubts are being raised regarding the self-organizing capacities of largely autonomous higher-education institutions to assure and protect the quality of their performances. It is, for instance, argued that the dominant accreditation systems only address minimum quality levels and disregard incentives for excellence. In addition, the dominant governance approaches are accused of stimulating processes of introversion (for instance, through the dominance of peer review in quality-assurance processes), thus creating a lack of transparency regarding the activities and performances of higher-education institutions. A second point of critique addresses the imminent drive toward homogeneity in higher-education systems. The uniformity of governmental "framework-only" steering, combined with the large autonomy of higher-education institutions, creates substantial opportunities for imitation and stimulates "academic drift" and an inefficient "reputation race," leading to a decrease in the levels of diversity in higher-education systems (van Vught 2008).

As a reaction to this criticism, a new view on higher-education governance appears to be developing. The main focus of this new approach is on transparency, in particular the transparency of the activities and performances of higher-education institutions for their various groups of clients.

Information Asymmetry

The basic theoretical notion behind the increasing interest in transparency in higher education stems from an economic analysis of higher education as an experience good or maybe even a credence good. An experience good is one whose quality can only be judged after consuming it. This stands in contrast to the textbook case of "search goods" whose quality can be judged by consumers in advance. In the case of credence goods, consumers do not know the quality of the good even after consumption (Bonroy and Constantatos 2008; Dulleck and Kerschbamer 2006). Examples of credence goods (or "trust goods") include doctor consultations and computer repairs.

The subjective quality of higher education cannot be known to clients in advance, which makes it an experience good. Whether or not students really know how good the teaching has been in enhancing their knowledge, skills, and competencies (and whether higher education is thus a credence good) is a subject of debate. But we may safely assume that higher-education clients cannot know the quality of services to be provided beforehand (van Vught and Westerheijden 2012).

The phenomenon of experience or credence goods is inherent in services, the production of which takes place in the interaction between supplier and client. Nevertheless, it is helpful for future clients to know in more detail what is being offered and how previous or current clients value the service. Each client or consumer may be unique, but clients also have common characteristics and might even share needs and satisfaction. However, such information is not always readily available. Hence, tools that provide transparency may help counteract information deficiencies between suppliers and clients. This holds true not just for students, but also for other stakeholders in higher education such as companies, representatives of professions, and governments.

From their professional perspective, academics argue that they know better than any other stakeholder what it takes to deliver a high-quality higher education—and they have a case. But this view also implies that a principal agent like asymmetry of information exists, which may tempt higher-education institutions not to maximize the quality of their education services, and even to show opportunistic behaviour. For instance, universities may exploit the information asymmetries to cross-subsidize research activity using resources intended for teaching (Massy 1996).

The combination of information asymmetries and potential client ignorance has led to corrective actions with the intention of preventing providers from taking advantage of clients. Regulation—by government or the providers themselves—aims to protect clients and/or providers. This can include rules on service quality, conditions imposed on providers, or the supply of information. Accreditation, quality assessment, student guides, and listings of recognized providers are some of the obvious examples from the higher-education field. However, it is not necessarily government that undertakes these actions. Monitoring, screening, signalling, and selection can also take place through quality-inspection agencies, acting independently of the government or created by the providers themselves.

In principle, there are many ways in which transparency can be increased. Information problems can be tackled through certificates, standards (e.g., ISO), guarantees, or insurance and rules relating to consumer protection. The information asymmetries are also what transparency tools such as report cards, quality-assurance mechanisms, rankings, and league tables often seek to tackle. Alternatively, systems that link a university's performance to the budget it receives are not only intended to protect clients but, by giving more weight to accountability, also try to ensure that the social benefit of higher education is stressed. Performance contracts are an example of stronger transparency tools. Further on in this chapter these performance contracts will be discussed in more detail.

Networked Governance

A recent conceptual approach called "networked governance" is of special relevance to our discussion of transparency in higher education. Networked governance is a combination of the state-supervisory model (with substantial institutional autonomy) and a new focus on clients. In this emerging governance approach, higher-education institutions negotiate with their stakeholders (including students, government authorities, and so on) about the services they will provide.

Networked governance has emerged out of the new public management paradigm of governance, which dominated throughout most of the 1990s. It has changed its perspective from a focus on efficiency and effectiveness toward incorporating objectives such as achieving social equity, creating societal impact (in terms of focusing on relevance and producing value from knowledge), and addressing the diverse needs of clientele. Where traditional public management stresses the contribution of higher-education institutions to producing public goods, the networked approach focuses on providing "public value." A networked approach also relies heavily on negotiation, collaboration, and partnerships, and much less on a one-size-fits-all approach.

From the perspective of networked governance, creating public value is the objective. The concept of public value emphasizes the creation of societal relevance. In the context of higher-education governance, the focus is on the co-creation of education and research by higher-education institutions together with their relevant stakeholders while keeping an eye on the individual needs of client groups (Bennington and Moore 2011; Stoker 2006).

Government nevertheless remains a key actor in this governance model. The "supervisory government" will want to be assured that national interests are served and client interests (in particular those of students) are protected. This implies some limitation on the autonomy of higher-education institutions, and leads to renewed demands for accountability. Government will also want to make sure that for all concerned there is a sufficient degree of transparency about the quality of the services delivered by higher-education institutions, allowing negotiations and the buildup of trust to take place.

Over the last three decades, some new policy instruments have been devised that clearly fit into this perspective of networked governance, and that allow clients to attain more transparency about the value and quality delivered by higher-education institutions. Performance contracts are a clear example of these new policy tools.

Performance Contracts

Performance contracts are agreements between the government and individual higher-education institutions, which set out specific goals that institutions will seek to achieve in a given time period. They specify intentions to accomplish given targets, measured against pre-set, known standards. Performance is deemed to be the fulfillment of an obligation specified in the contract. In contemporary higher education we can find these kinds of agreements under different labels and headings, including "compacts" (Australia, Ireland), "target agreements" (some German states), "outcome agreements" (Scotland), and "development plans" (Hong Kong, Denmark).

It should be pointed out that performance contracts are not similar to performance-based funding models. Performance-based funding is a type of funding where the (public) budget of a higher-education institution varies with the performance of that institution. In many higher-education systems, funding formulas are used to determine the public budget that institutions will receive. The performance of an institution is (one of the elements) fed into the formula to calculate the budget.

Frequently used performance indicators in the performance-based funding models are:

- Number of bachelor's and master's degrees and graduates
- Number of exams passed or credits earned by students
- Number of students from under-represented groups
- Study duration
- Number of PhD graduates
- Research productivity
- Research performance in terms of winning (research council) contracts
- Third-party income
- Revenues from knowledge transfers

In addition, some less frequently used performance indicators are:

- Internationalization (number of foreign students or staff)
- Quality of education based on student surveys
- Employability indicators (e.g., the number of employed graduates)
- Research quality and impact

Similar indicators can be and are being used in performance contracts. However, a crucial difference is that in performance contracts (unlike in performance-based funding models) the selection of the indicators is based on an agreement between the government or funding agency and the higher-education institutions.

What is judged to be a relevant performance measure is often a matter of discussion—sometimes, even a matter of opinion. In general, a crucial aspect of public value in higher education concerns the quality of the services provided by higher-education institutions. The measure-

ment of higher-education quality is thus an important focus of performance contracts. Quality measurement takes place by means of performance indicators that are goal-oriented, results-based, and can be
measured against pre-set standards.

A related issue concerns the choice of quantitative and/or qualitative indicators. A strong focus on quantitative measures has its attrac-
tions. They can be smart, transparent, and create a sense of objectivity (although they are not value-neutral). Assessment of performance
based on quantitative measures is also relatively easy. However, there
are also disadvantages. For one thing, only what gets measured gets
done. In addition, institutions may be encouraged to concentrate on
easy targets. The appeal of qualitative measures is that some relevant,
non-quantifiable issues can be addressed. The downside of using qualitative measures is that they are usually less clear and transparent, that
the transaction costs are relatively high, and that disputes may arise
over when the realization of qualitative targets needs to be assessed.

There are several aspects that further characterize performance contracts. One relevant question is whether the contract implies the pre-
scription of a certain set of outcomes (results that have to be achieved)
or only indicates the need for a higher-education institution to make
an effort to try to realize these outcomes. This is the difference between
"hard" and "soft" contracts.

A second set of issues is related to the funding dimension of the
contracts. Are performance contracts necessarily coupled with public
funding? Can one speak of performance contracts if no funding consequences are attached? If there is no funding linked to the agreements,
it would be better to speak of letters of intent instead of performance
contracts. Letters of intent would imply that the partners agree to focus
on certain activities (i.e., make a serious effort) with the aim of accom-
plishing particular goals, but without direct financial consequences. A
related issue concerns the question of how much funding should be
attached to performance contracts. Experience shows that even small
amounts can have a serious impact on institutional behaviour. However, if amounts are small in relation to the efforts to be made by the
institution, and the institution has an opportunity to acquire funds elsewhere, the impact on institutional behaviour is likely to be limited. A
related funding issue is to what extent performance contracts should
bring additional funding to institutions or whether the funding should
be siphoned from an existing budget. On the one hand, there is an argument to be made that attaching additional funding to performance

contracts creates a meaningful incentive for institutions to accept the contracts and to make an extra effort. On the other hand, public funds usually are scarce. Making a proportion of existing funding conditional on goal achievement is a more realistic option.

A third crucial aspect of performance contracts concerns the question of to what extent they should be made with the higher-education sector as a whole, its subsectors, or individual institutions. In principle, bilateral agreements with individual institutions are suitable for tailor-made contracts that will then, to some degree, differ from one institution to the other. For the aim of establishing a diversified higher-education system, or for optimally supporting the strengths of existing institutions, this appears to be a promising feature. Contracts addressing the entire sector bear the risk of all institutions moving in the same direction, thus creating system homogeneity. Tailor-made contracts, however, have high transaction costs and require that the government have the capacity to monitor and assess the consequences of the different contracts for the system as a whole.

As indicated, the most crucial aspect of performance contracts is that they are a joint undertaking. In line with the conceptual perspective of networked governance, reaching consensus between the contract partners (government and higher-education institutions) and involving clients and stakeholders throughout the process are highly important for the contracts to be effective.

While the government may be in the driver's seat (e.g., developing guidelines and templates), serious institutional involvement in the process is a necessary condition for the successful development and implementation of the contracts. This implies that these institutions should not only be able to voice their interests and negotiate the contents of the contracts, but also express their ambitions and ideas based on their specific profiles and strategies. Institutions should have the opportunity to discuss, from their own strategic positions, the various objectives, targets, and indicators in the contracts, and agree on the selections to be made. They should have ample room to explore the contract contents with their own clients and stakeholder groups and feel sufficiently supported by these groups to accept the contract conditions. As such, they should see themselves as "co-owners" of the contracts.

The governmental actors have the crucial responsibility to represent national policy objectives, and to protect the general client interests that may be under pressure from the negative characteristics of information asymmetry and possible client ignorance. Government will first of all see itself as responsible for sufficient levels of transparency concerning the performances of the higher-education institutions. In this respect, government is the partner in the performance contracts that has a focus on overall system quality and public value. In this role, government will want to be assured that the quality of higher-education services is measured and reported.

A major challenge in higher-education performance contracts is how quality measurement is addressed and operationalized. Given that the contracts are a joint undertaking, consensus must be reached between government and the higher-education institutions about the indicators used to measure quality. In addition, these indicators should allow sufficient levels of diversity regarding institutional profiles and reflect the interests and ambitions of the various stakeholders and clients of the individual institutions.

It is highly doubtful whether a set of final and universal quality indicators can ever be defined. The definition of quality remains contested in the higher-education literature (D'Andrea 2007). Agreement appears to exist only about a definition as "fitness for purpose" (Harvey and Green 1993), which may imply that there are as many qualities as there are purposes of stakeholders. In this sense, quality is a relative concept. Several decades of trying to define the quality of higher education have so far not led to a definitive conclusion. If quality definitions and goals are highly contextual, finding a definite set of indicators to measure quality is an illusion. Reaching consensus on a specific (contextual) set of quality indicators may be the best way to make sure that quality is being seriously addressed in performance contracts.

During the last decade, performance contracts have begun to find their way into national higher-education governance systems in several countries around the world. Governments have chosen different approaches to designing and implementing these contracts. Some of these approaches are closer to the general aspects just described than others. In the following section, a case study is presented on the use of performance contracts in the higher-education system of the Netherlands.

Performance Contracts in the Netherlands: Process and Results

The Netherlands has a binary higher-education system with two subsectors: the research universities (eighteen in total, including four denominational universities and an Open University) and thirty-eight universities of applied sciences (UAS), or *hogescholen* in Dutch. Both are publicly funded. More than one-third of the students (about 260,000) attend research universities and nearly two-thirds (about 450,000 students), studying primarily for bachelor-level degrees, attend UAS. There are also independent, private higher-education institutions (about seventy) that do not receive government funding, have relatively few students, and conduct little research.

Particularly in terms of research performance, the Dutch higher-education system is, internationally speaking, of high quality. Dutch universities perform very well in terms of research output and impact. However, given the ambitions of the Dutch government, concerns have been expressed about the efficiency of the higher-education system and about relatively low completion rates. A major concern is a lack of diversity at the system level; higher-education institutions show little diversity in their institutional profiles, including in terms of the different categories of students to whom they cater.

For a long time, the public funding of universities and *hogescholen* was primarily based on formula funding, with a mix of input funding (student numbers, historical allocations) and performance-based funding elements (number of degrees at the bachelor's, master's, and PhD levels).

Since 2012, a small portion of the funding for higher-education institutions has been based on performance contracts. This reform replaced an earlier trial of collective contract funding, in which contracts were signed with both the university sector and the UAS sector as a whole. The experience with these collective agreements (in place from 2008 to 2011) at the subsystem level showed that they were not sufficiently aligned with the strategic targets of the higher-education institutions involved and had very little impact.

The introduction of performance contracts came about as a result of recommendations by a special committee on the future sustainability of the Dutch higher-education system, known as the Veerman committee (named after its chair). The Veerman report stated that, given the Dutch government's ambition to be among the most competitive knowledge economies worldwide, the Dutch higher-education system was not future-proof. The dropout rate was too high, students were not properly challenged, and there was too little flexibility in the system to serve the various needs of students and the labour market. Its main recommendation was that a long-term strategy was needed to improve the quality and diversity of Dutch higher education. This was to be realized by encouraging higher-education institutions to bolster their individual profiles on the basis of their strengths in education and research, stimulating differentiation in the range of programs offered (two-year associate degrees, more master's degree programs to be offered by UAS), and opening the possibility for the selection of students at entrance. The committee also recommended a gradual reduction in the share of student-based (input) funding in favour of (performance-related) mission-based funding. Relatively good performances in line with strategic institutional missions were to be rewarded. Mission-based funding should be operationalized by means of performance contracts requiring the higher-education institutions to make "crystal clear agreements with the government regarding their performances in improving the education they provide" (Veerman Committee 2010).

The Veerman report was widely accepted by all actors involved in Dutch higher education: Parliament, the minister, the higher-education institutions, students, and employer organizations. The majority of its suggestions were included in the ministry's Strategic Agenda for Higher Education, Research and Science, which was published in July 2011. This Strategic Agenda expressed the need to strengthen the strategic dialogue and revise the funding system. Performance contracts were to be made with individual higher-education institutions (both universities of applied sciences and research universities).

The performance of higher-education institutions was to be financially rewarded. In the funding model, some 7 percent of educational funding was set aside for this component. Extra financial resources were made available for this "quality and profiling budget." The legal basis for the performance agreements proved difficult, but it was acknowledged that the agreements were to be seen as an experiment and evaluated after the first round (2013–2016).

In December 2011, a general agreement was signed between the two university associations and the ministry of education. The associations representing the research universities and the UAS pledged to enter into contracts to work on improving the quality of education and sharpening their profiles. Through these agreements, the institutions committed themselves to the system of performance contracts. The ministry committed itself to creating the proper legal and financial conditions required for realizing the ambitions in the performance contracts.

In order to work out the idea of the performance contracts, the higher-education institutions were invited to deliver their individual strategic plans. These did not have an obligatory format. The only condition was that institutions were obliged to formulate their own specific 2015 targets for seven agreed-upon indicators related to improved educational quality and achievement (see below).

In May 2012, all higher-education institutions submitted a plan (a profile document) for a four-year performance contract with the ministry. The proposals listed the institution's individual ambitions for the years 2012–2015 in terms of improving its educational achievement, strengthening its education and research profile, and increasing the impact and utilization of academic and practice-oriented research.

The budget at stake was 7 percent of the annual teaching grant for 2013–2016. This consisted of 5 percent for a conditional budget (conditional on the signing of the performance contract, and continued after 2016 on the condition that the 2015 performance targets were achieved) and 2 percent for a selective budget (a competitive fund awarding more funding for the best proposals; "best" was primarily judged in terms of differentiation and concentration). The proposals did not just list quantitative targets, but also contained the strategic foundations and concrete plans that explained the higher-education institutions' activities for profile and educational enhancement.

A crucial aspect of the performance contracts was a set of seven agreed-upon quality indicators, covering teaching performance, excellence, and "dedicated actions." The indicators were assumed to address both educational quality and educational achievement. The selection of these indicators was part of the general agreements signed earlier by the two university associations. Most of these indicators were already in use. They were as follows:

- Completion rate for bachelor students enrolling in the second year of study
- Dropout rate in first-year bachelor's programs
- Students changing study program in first-year bachelor's programs
- An education excellence indicator (see below)
- Teacher quality (for research universities, percentage of teachers holding teaching certificates; for UAS, percentage of teachers with a master's and/or PhD degree)
- Educational intensity (number of face-to-face teaching contact hours per week in the first year of a study program)
- Indirect costs (i.e., academic staff/support staff ratio and overheads as percentage of turnover)

To indicate excellence in education, there were two options. First, an institution could use the "participation of students in excellence routes" as an indicator. This could refer to specific tracks that had been validated in the earlier national policy context of excellence stimulation, or to tracks still to be developed by the institution. In the latter case, an external validation of the program would have to be sought in due time (no later than 2013). Secondly, an institution was offered the possibility of choosing from two other indicators expressing education excellence: the institution's student satisfaction scores in the National Student Survey or the accreditation agency's ratings of an institution's degree programs.

Over the duration of the contracts, the quality indicators have increasingly become a topic of debate. From the very beginning the national student associations indicated that they felt insufficiently involved in the indicator selection process. Also the UAS association and several individual institutional leaders argued that the agreed-upon indicators did not sufficiently address the relevant quality issues and were too focused on educational efficiency.

In January 2012, an independent review committee was appointed to evaluate the proposals by the higher-education institutions and advise the minister. Where there was a positive evaluation of an institution's proposal, the minister would, in principle, be prepared to sign a performance contract with the institution.

The review committee scored the proposals using three criteria:

1. Ambition (the level of ambition, combined with a "reality check")

2. Alignment (the contribution of the proposals to national policy objectives in terms of diversity and their fit with the national and European innovation agendas)

3. Feasibility (whether the proposals for differentiation and concentration were sufficiently operationalized in concrete plans)

In November 2012, the committee's evaluations were submitted to the minister who then translated the evaluation scores into a performance budget. As discussed earlier, the institution's performance budget consisted of two parts: 5 percent conditional funding and 2 percent selective funding.

Performance contracts were concluded with all publicly funded higher-education institutions, implying that all institutional plans were judged to be of sufficient quality. From 2013 on, the review committee carried out annual monitoring of the progress made by the institutions in terms of their achievement of performance targets. In 2014, the review committee also undertook a mid-term review to establish whether the selective funding should continue for the remaining two years of the four-year period.

In 2016, the review committee assessed whether the targets were met. The committee evaluated the performances in all contracts and held (as at the start and during the mid-term of the process) "critical friend" discussions with the leadership of each institution. By the end of 2016, the committee presented its final assessments to the minister. All but six institutions (all UAS) had performed sufficiently; seven institutions (four research universities and three UAS) had even realized all of their ambitions. The minister followed the committee's advice and decided on the financial consequences of the contracts, which entailed a small budgetary increase for the better performing institutions, and some minor reductions for the underperforming institutions.

The overall results of the process appeared to be impressive. Politicians and employers expressed their appreciation and the national media reported that the Dutch higher-education system had taken a major step forward. The results in terms of quality and study success can be summarized as follows:

- Higher levels of student satisfaction in both sectors (research universities and UAS)
- Higher numbers of students in "excellence tracks"
- All programs showing at least twelve contact hours per week
- Higher percentage of teachers in UAS with a master's and/or PhD degree
- Nearly all teachers in research universities having a teaching certificate
- Substantial decrease in indirect costs
- Increase in bachelor's program completion rates in research universities (not in UAS)
- Decrease in dropout rates in research universities (remaining constant in UAS)
- Slight decrease in student program change in UAS (remaining constant in research universities)

In addition, the diversity of the educational programs in terms of intake and outflow levels, target groups, and educational provision had increased. And although there appeared to be little change in the institutional portfolios of educational programs, these outcomes were interpreted as an indication of increasing diversity at the system level. The research portfolios of the research institutions showed a trend toward a broader coverage of research fields in all institutions, and a more equal distribution of publication output between institutions. The UAS's research activities appeared to have focused increasingly on applied research and regional knowledge transfer.

In its final system report, the review committee concluded that the performance contracts appeared to have had a major impact on the Dutch higher-education system. The quality and efficiency levels of the system (as measured by the agreed-upon indicators) had increased, there were clear initiatives for institutional educational profiling leading to the beginning of an increase in system-level diversity, there was a growing alignment with national policy targets, and transparency at both system and institutional levels had increased. The committee recommended that the contracts should be continued as mutual agreements between government and individual institutions, that they should continue to have financial consequences, and that the financial incentives should be meticulous and appropriate. In addition, the committee suggested that the performance contracts should be kept simple and that indicators should be relevant, valid, actionable, and reliable (Higher Education and Research Review Committee 2016).

Regarding the selection of the agreed-upon indicators, the committee noted a lack of consensus. Time pressure in the early phase of the process had led to a set of indicators for educational quality and achievement, which, during the process, was increasingly seen by both student associations and some institutions as too rigid. In addition, the various stakeholders and clients of the institutions were hardly involved in the selection process. The committee argued that, given the fact that no final set of quality indicators exists, in the future ample time should be taken to reach consensus about a set of agreed-upon indicators. Furthermore, the committee recommended that this number of universal indicators should be kept to a minimum, that the institutions should have sufficient choice regarding their own quality indicators, that institutional clients and stakeholders should be strongly involved in the indicator selection process, and that the specific contexts of individual institutions should continue to be taken into account.

The future of the performance agreements is still a topic of debate. As a result of recent reforms in the student support system, extra funds will become available for the higher-education sector in the coming years. Parliament agreed to these reforms on the condition that the extra funds would be invested in further improving the quality of teaching and learning. To ensure that institutions will work on realizing this, a next generation of performance contracts has been suggested. Whether these new contracts will be largely similar to those in the first round is still to be determined, but it does seem clear that in future years the agenda for higher education will continue to be discussed on the basis of bilateral contracts between the ministry and the institutions.

References

Bennington, John, and Mark H. Moore, eds. 2011. *Public Value: Theory and Practice*, London and New York: Palgrave Macmillan.

de Boer, H., J. Enders, J. File, and B. Jongbloed. 2010. *Governance Reform: Progress in Higher Education Reform Across Europe*, Volume 1: Executive Summary and Main Report. Brussels: European Commission.

Bonroy, Olivier, and Christos Constantatos. 2008. "On the Use of Labels in Credence Goods Markets." *Journal of Regulatory Economics* 33 (3), 237–52. https://doi.org/10.1007/s11149-008-9058-z

Clark, Burton R. 1983. *The Higher Education System: Academic Organization in Cross-National Perspective*. Berkeley: University of California Press.

D'Andrea, Vaneeta-Marie. 2007. "Improving Teaching and Learning in Higher Education: Can Learning Theory Add Value to Quality Reviews?" In *Quality Assurance in Higher Education*, edited by Don Westerheijden, Bjorn Stensaker, and Maria Joao Rosa. 209–223. Dordrecht: Springer Netherlands.

Dill, David D. 1992. "Quality by Design: Toward a Framework for Academic Quality Management." In *Higher Education: Handbook of Theory and Research*, Vol. VIII, edited by John Smart. New York: Agathon Press.

Dulleck, Uwe, and Rudolph Kerschbamer. 2006. "On Doctors, Mechanics, and Computer Specialists: The Economics of Credence Goods." *Journal of Economic Literature* 44 (1), 5–42.

Harvey, Lee, and Diana Green. 1993. "Defining Quality." *Assessment & Evaluation in Higher Education* 18 (1), 9–34.

Higher Education and Research Review Committee. 2016. *System Report 2016*. The Hague: Netherlands. http://www.rcho.nl/images/Stelsel rapportage-Reviewcommissie-2016-Engels.pdf

Neave, Guy, and Frans A. van Vught, eds. 1991. *Prometheus Bound: The Changing Relationship Between Government and Higher Education in*

Western Europe. London: Pergamon.

Massy, William F., ed. 1996. *Resource Allocation in Higher Education.* Ann Arbor: The University of Michigan Press.

Stoker, Gerry. 2006. "Public Value Management. A New Narrative for Networked Governance?" *The American Review of Public Administration* 36 (1), 41–57.

van Vught, Frans A., ed. 1989. *Governmental Strategies and Innovation in Higher Education.* London: Jessica Kingsley.

———. 2008. "Mission Diversity and Reputation in Higher Education." *Higher Education Policy* 21 (2), 151–74.

van Vught, Frans A., and Don F. Westerheijden. 2012. "Transparency, Quality and Accountability." In *Multidimensional Ranking: The Design and Development of U-Multirank,* edited by Frans A. van Vught and Frank Ziegele, 11–23. Dordrecht: Springer.

Veerman Committee. 2010. *Commissie Toekomstbestendig Hoger Onderwijsstelsel, Differentieren in Drievoud.* Ministry of Education. The Hague: Netherlands (in Dutch). https://www.asva.nl/sites/default/files/pages/2011/adv-cie-toekomstbestendig-ho.pdf

7

Benchmarking Higher-Education System Performance: A Look at Learning and Teaching

Cláudia S. Sarrico

Why Look at Higher-Education System Performance?

Higher education contributes to economic progress by improving human capital and innovation, and spurring wider social, cultural, and environmental development. As a result, as economies have developed, higher education has rapidly expanded. This growth reflects its benefits to individuals and society. However, there are questions about how well higher education is performing and these concerns put pressure on higher-education systems to improve (OECD 2017).

The Performance of the Education Function

So far, most measures of higher-education performance have focused on study success as measured by retention, progression and completion rates, and time-to-degree (European Commission 2015). Comparing these measures across systems gives us, at best, a measure of how efficient or productive systems are, but says little about the quality of graduate learning outcomes.

The use of these measures, in effect productivity measures, can also have a perverse effect on equity. If compared in a crude way, they will penalize institutions and systems with strong policies aimed at broadening access. As systems move from elite to mass higher education, the heterogeneity of the student body will need to be taken into account when assessing study success.

Simply using indicators of observed performance is not enough. The correct approach takes into account the difference between observed performance and expected performance, given the characteristics of the student intake in terms of socio-economic background and prior attainment (Johnes and Taylor 1990; *The Economist* 2017). However, such measures are often not provided because the data are not available.

Using measures of study success, as those described above, assumes that the quality of learning outcomes is generally the same across higher education. It is unlikely that this assumption was ever true, but now with increasing massification and diversity of higher education, it is highly doubtful.

Several systems, such as those in Australia, England, Ontario, and across Europe, are developing projects to measure learning outcomes and even learning gains (Barrie et al. 2014; Weingarten 2014; Goff et al. 2015; Wagenaar forthcoming).

The OECD's Programme for International Student Assessment (PISA) compares the educational attainment of 15-year-old students worldwide. So far, no comparable program to PISA exists to evaluate higher-education systems by testing the learning outcomes of graduates. Schleicher (2015) presents the problem well: "Without data on learning outcomes, judgements about the quality of teaching and learning at higher education institutions will continue to be made on the basis of flawed rankings, derived not from outcomes, nor even outputs— but from idiosyncratic inputs and reputation surveys."

Higher education has expanded enormously and so has the cost of providing it. Austerity measures have affected some systems in response to the 2008 financial crisis, and competing demands for other services often prompted countries to seek measures to make their systems more affordable.

Johnstone and Marcucci (2007) track trends, such as increasing unit costs of instruction, increasing enrolments, and faltering government tax revenues, which show how financing higher education is a challenge. Some solutions aimed at reducing costs (such as increasing the casualization of academic staff, student-staff ratios, and teaching loads) may negatively affect the quality of the education provided and the equity of outcomes.

Other solutions (such as diversifying the system, mergers, the use of technology in teaching and learning, and cost-sharing measures) may increase the sustainability of systems in the long run by making it more affordable and ensuring adequate levels of funding.

For higher-education systems, short-term cost considerations should not be prioritized over the outcomes and long-term value that the system provides in improving human capital, economic growth, and social development.

The affordability challenge of higher education is increasingly moving from simple economic considerations, cost containment, and adequate levels of funding to more complex questions regarding value for money.

The discussion of value for money goes beyond simply cost, and focuses on the cost-effectiveness of the system, taking into consideration the outcomes attained given the cost of the system. Weingarten et al. (2015) analyze equity of access, the value to students, and the value to society obtained from the investment per student for each province in Canada. Their conclusion is that more funding does not necessarily equate with better equity and outcomes.

Governments have made widespread efforts to increase equity of access by increasing the number of places available at existing institutions, increasing the number and nature of institutions, diversifying the program offerings, and making a concerted effort to reach under-represented groups. By many measures, these policies have been successful in improving equity of access. However, there is evidence that equity of access has not been accompanied by a commensurate improvement in equity of outcomes, with many of these students failing to complete their studies (Galindo-Rueda and Vignoles 2005; Quinn 2013; Eurydice 2014).

The Way Forward

Performance in higher education has been focused on individual institutions as measured in rankings. However, international rankings are mostly based on input and reputation measures and they have produced well-documented perverse effects, such as biasing systems towards research performance to the detriment of learning and teaching (Hazelkorn 2015). As Hazelkorn (2017) puts it: "Pursuit of excellence is measured in terms of achievements of individual universities rather than the system or society collectively; in other words, it promotes world-class universities rather than world-class systems."

To counteract this problem, the focus of performance measurement and management in higher education should move from the higher-education institution to the system as the unit of analysis. The system includes all higher-education institutions and not just universities, and all levels of higher education, from associate degree to doctorate.

The current focus on study success is not enough. The debate can no longer be just about the efficiency of the system, because both efficiency and effectiveness matter. This means addressing not only the quantity of graduates a system produces, but also the quality of graduate outcomes. Graduate outcomes most obviously relate to learning outcomes and learning gains directly obtained from higher education. But graduate outcomes also reflect the effect of higher education on the labour market and social outcomes of graduates.

In addition, the effectiveness of the system relates not only to the quality of graduate outcomes, but also the equity of outcomes; that is, how outcomes are distributed among social groups. Monitoring equity in higher education will mean tracking students in their trajectory through higher education—from applicant, to student, graduate, employee, and citizen—rather than just tracking participation rates. This will mean having disaggregated data by groups of interest, based on age, gender, socio-economic status, ethnicity, migrant status, disability status, indigeneity, rural provenance, etc.

It is not enough to know the results of higher education; if we are going to enhance the performance of higher-education systems, we need to act on the determinants of those results. For that we need to understand the levers of better performance. What practices in higher education drive better student learning and graduate outcomes?

This requires going beyond analyzing administrative and registry data on enrolments, progression, and graduations. It involves dedicated surveys of the student experience, such as the National Survey of Student Engagement (NSSE) in the United States (McCormick, Kinzie, and Gonyea 2013).

Students are very important stakeholders in the higher-education system, but they are by no means the only ones. Surveying other actors will improve our understanding of what practices drive improvement. This will mean dedicated surveys not only of students, but also of staff, graduates, and employers. These surveys exist, but mostly at the institutional level, rarely at the system level, and hardly at all at the international level. As discussed above, no PISA equivalent exists for higher education. And equally, higher education has no equivalent of TALIS, the OECD's Teaching and Learning International Survey, which surveys teachers and school leaders.

Student surveys will give us information about student characteristics, student experience, and student engagement. Staff surveys that include non-academic staff, will give us information about practices regarding required qualifications, recruitment, employment and working conditions, duties, promotion, remuneration, working practices, staff appraisal, professional development, and staff satisfaction. Graduate surveys will give us information about skill proficiency and skill use, labour market outcomes, and social outcomes. Employer surveys will give us information about satisfaction with graduate skills, mismatches and gaps in skills, training opportunities and practices, expectations, satisfaction, and expected trends in the labour market.

Knowing what happens in the learning and teaching process of higher education—through systematically surveying the actors, and seeing how that correlates with better graduate outcomes—will give us a better understanding of what works and what does not.

A Benchmarking Approach to Enhancing Higher-Education Performance

A benchmarking approach to enhancing higher-education system performance is one way to address the issues discussed so far in this chapter. In this approach, the performance of each system is compared to the observed performance of other systems. By going beyond metrics to also focus on policy and practice benchmarking, it can better help tell the story behind the performance of higher-education systems. And it will enable cross-country comparisons and peer learning to support the developmental dimension of performance measurement and management, and inform higher-education policy design, implementation, and evaluation.

The OECD project on benchmarking higher-education system performance will collect and analyze data and information on higher-education systems through regular rounds of benchmarking exercises using this approach. Comparing the performance of the different higher-education systems, and how different policies and practices appear to be driving that performance will provide the basis for policy recommendations.

With time, longitudinal analysis will help us evaluate how higher-education policies in different systems steer performance-enhancing practices.

The Model

The OECD developed a conceptual framework for benchmarking higher-education system performance with a system-performance model that takes into account: (i) the three functions of higher education: education, research, and engagement; (ii) the whole production process, from input, activity, and output to outcome; (iii) the context within which systems operate, from the wider economic, social, and cultural context to the policies steering the higher-education system; and (iv) the full span of performance, from relevance to value and sustainability (Figure 7.1).

Higher-education systems are part of an economic, social, and cultural environment—an environment with needs in terms of human capital, and wider economic, social, cultural, and environmental development. These needs prompt action by governments, which will define policies and objectives for higher education with relevant stakeholders. The extent to which the objectives of higher education address the needs of society gives a measure of its relevance.

Higher education transforms inputs into outputs, which in turn produce outcomes. Inputs take the form of the financial and human resources allocated to the higher-education system. These provide the resources for the activities of learning and teaching, research, and engagement with the wider world. These activities produce the outputs of higher education such as graduates. A look at the cost of funding higher education will give a measure of the economy of the system. Looking at the outputs produced given the inputs available will provide measures of efficiency; that is, how productive the system is.

Outputs will produce effects in the form of intermediate outcomes, which are more directly attributable to the performance of the higher-education system such as the learning outcomes of graduates. The intermediate outcomes eventually lead to final outcomes, such as the labour market and social outcomes of graduates, which will be a product of the performance of the system in conjunction with contextual factors that the system cannot fully control.

The quality of outcomes and how equitably they are distributed among different population groups will provide measures of the

Figure 7.1

OECD Higher-education System Performance Model

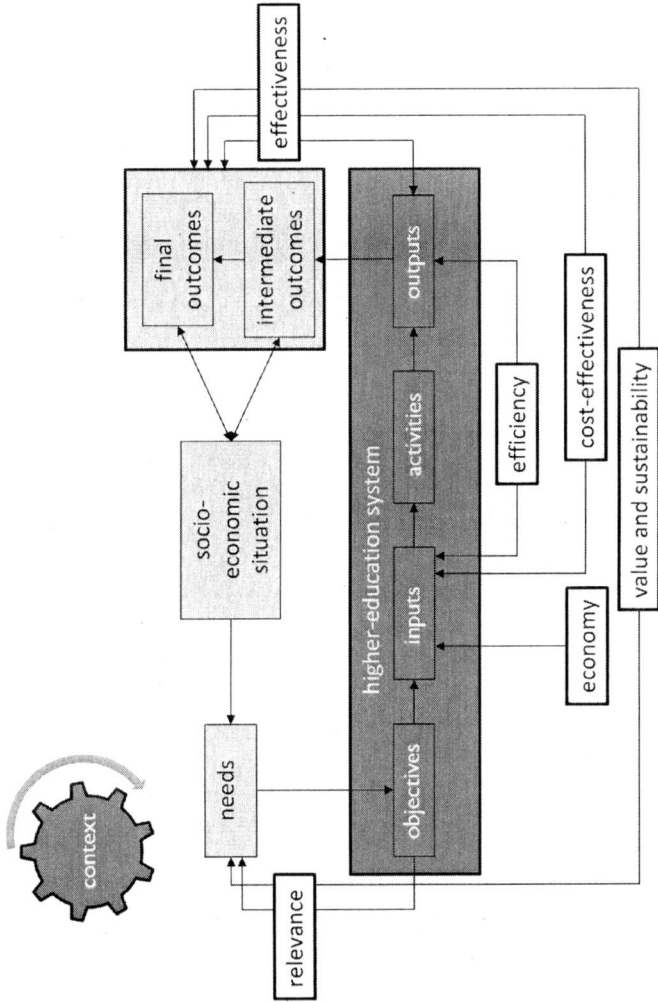

Source: Adapted from OECD (2017).

effectiveness of the system. How much it costs to achieve that level of effectiveness, and how it compares to other systems, provides a cost-effectiveness analysis.

How final outcomes ultimately address the needs of society will give a measure of the value of the system and its sustainability in the long run.

Applying the model to the education function of higher education means answering a number of questions including the following:

Effectiveness:

Is the higher-education system adding value to human capital?

- Have graduates received a significant learning gain from their higher-education experience?
- Do graduates reach the intended learning outcomes and the associated skills proficiency?
- Do graduates achieve the intended labour market outcomes in terms of participation rate, appropriate job levels, and earning premiums?
- Do graduates gain the expected social outcomes, such as good health, active citizenship, and life satisfaction?
- Are the outcomes equitably distributed among different demographic groups (in terms of socio-economic background, age, ethnicity, migration status, disability, etc.)?

Efficiency:

Can the higher-education system deliver its intended outputs with available resources? Can the system be more productive without hindering effectiveness (quality and equity) through the following:

- Increasing retention rates, progression rates, and completion rates
- Decreasing time-to-completion
- Operating at a higher ratio of students to staff

Economy:

Is the system receiving adequate funding to allow it to operate at an efficient and effective level? How much funding is higher education receiving? Is there scope for cost savings in the system without hindering effectiveness through the following:

- Consolidation of higher-education networks (mergers), or associated facilities such as libraries, laboratories, student and staff accommodation, sports facilities, etc.
- Better system procurement policies (e.g., for informatics equipment, for access to research databases, etc.)
- Adequate collective bargaining arrangements for staff compensation

Can costs be controlled through measures such as:

- Caps on student numbers, tuition fees, *numerus clausus*
- Limiting the number of institutions and degree programs
- Predefined national salary scales
- Transparent funding formulas indexed to inflation or other indexes
- Limiting those eligible for student loans or grants
- Promoting the specialization of institutions (by level of education, field of study, research versus teaching orientation, basic versus applied research orientation)
- Targeted funding for agreed delivery

Can costs be shared to lighten the burden on the public budget through measures such as:

- Introducing or raising tuition fees
- Introducing or raising tuition fees for international students
- Diversification of funding sources, including fees and earned income from continuing education, technology transfer, social engagement activities, philanthropy, and endowments

Data and Information

The conceptual framework above was translated into a data architecture to enable the benchmarking exercise. At that point, only conceptually relevant dimensions were considered without taking account of the availability of data. In the second phase, the OECD mapped comparable international data to the data architecture and identified gaps in the data. In the third phase, the OECD surveyed countries on the availability of national data to fill in those gaps. The identification of gaps in the data, and developments at the national level to address them will feed into the process of designing and implementing new, internationally comparable, higher-education indicators at the OECD, which will ultimately improve the benchmarking exercises.

Despite the gaps in available data, the number of metrics available is quite large. Four criteria were used to select metrics for the baseline analysis of the project: coverage, quality, comparability, and parsimony. The baseline analysis includes forty-seven metrics relevant for the education function, only four of which will be provided by the relevant national jurisdiction (shown in italics in Table 7.1); the remaining indicators are internationally available.

Metrics tell us about levels of performance in a number of dimensions but do not tell us the reasons behind the observed performance. The benchmarking project uses qualitative information about the structure and governance of higher education, the higher-education policies driving the system, and the practices emerging from the policies to analyze system performance. It asks key questions for each policy area to better understand the observed performance.

These questions look at the policy process in terms of design, implementation, and evaluation, and the policies themselves are classified under the four common types of policy levers (that is, regulation, funding, information, and organization) to better understand the reasons behind the observed performance:

- Who was involved in the following stages of the policy process: design, implementation, evaluation?
- What was the main purpose of the policy?
- Does the policy include measurable targets?
- Describe the policy in terms of the main policy levers used: regulations, funding, information, and organization.
- What practices did the policy lead to? (What practices appear to be making a difference? What practices do not appear to be making much of a difference? What practices have produced perverse effects?)
- How is the implementation of the policy monitored and its effectiveness assessed?
- Who are the stakeholders involved in the implementation and evaluation process? Are they the same or different from the ones involved in the design phase?

These questions are asked for a number of relevant policy areas in order to better understand the performance of the education function (see Figure 7.2 for an example).

… continued on page 139

Table 7.1

Baseline Education Metrics

Financial resources

    Expenditure on higher education as a percentage of GDP

    Public expenditure on higher education as a percentage of total public expenditure

    Relative proportion of public and private expenditure on higher education

    Annual expenditure per higher-education student on core educational services

    Distribution of current expenditure by resource category: compensation of teachers, compensation of other staff, other current expenditures

Human resources

    Ratio of students to teaching staff

    Distribution of academic staff at education level by age groups

    Percentage of full-time versus part-time staff

    Permanent versus non-permanent staff

    Average annual salaries of teachers in public institutions

Access

    Transition from upper secondary vocational education and training to postsecondary education

    Percentage of students enrolled part-time by age group

    Profile of first-time entrants, by gender, age, international status, level of education, and field of education

    First-time entrants by age group (to be estimated)

    Socio-economic background of students

    Skills on entry: use PISA scores as proxy

Internationalization

    International student mobility and foreign students

    Brain gain as share of international students who continue residing in the host country after graduation

Table 7.1, continued

Baseline Education Metrics

Graduation

First-time graduation rates, by tertiary level

Profile of first-time tertiary graduates, by gender, age, international status, level of education, field of study

Completion rate

Completion rate of full-time students by level of education, gender, and duration

Dropout rates

Attainment

Intergenerational mobility by educational attainment of parents and immigrant status

Percentage of adults who have attained tertiary education by type of program and age group

Field of education studied among tertiary-educated adults

Adult learning

Participation in employer sponsored education by educational attainment

Skills outcomes

Distribution of literacy proficiency levels, by educational attainment and gender

Distribution of numeracy proficiency levels, by educational attainment and gender

Distribution of skills and readiness to use information and communication technologies for problem solving, by educational attainment and gender

Measures of graduate skills use from PIAAC (such as use of ICT at work—to be estimated)

Educational attainment of youth neither employed nor in education or training

Level of the best-known foreign language (self-reported) by educational attainment level

Table 7.1, continued

Baseline Education Metrics

Labour market outcomes

Employment, unemployment and inactivity rates of 25–34 year olds by program orientation and educational attainment

Temporary employees by sex, age, and educational attainment level

Full-time and part-time employment by sex, age, and educational attainment

Self-employment by sex, age, and educational attainment level

Relative earnings of full-time, full-year workers by educational attainment

Private costs and benefits for a man attaining tertiary education

Private costs and benefits for a woman attaining tertiary education

Public costs and benefits for a man attaining tertiary education

Public costs and benefits for a woman attaining tertiary education

Current work—job satisfaction

Social outcomes

Percentage of adults reporting that they are in good health, by educational attainment, literacy proficiency level, and gender

Percentage of adults reporting that they volunteer at least once a month, by educational attainment, literacy proficiency level, and gender

Percentage of adults reporting that they trust others, by educational attainment, literacy proficiency level, and gender

Percentage of adults reporting that they believe they have a say in government, by educational attainment, literacy proficiency level, and gender

Life satisfaction

Note: For dimensions in italics only national data is available. For all other dimensions international comparable data is available.

Source: Adapted from OECD (2017).

Figure 7.2

Metric, and Policy and Practice Benchmarking of Education

Input
Profile of entrants
Expenditure per student

Activity
Ratio of student to teaching staff
International student mobility
Retention rates
Progression rates
Time to degree

Output
Profile of graduates
Completion rates

Outcome
Learning outcomes/gain
Skills proficiency levels
Proficiency in foreign language
Labour market outcomes
Social outcomes

Policy and Practice Benchmarking

| Access and participation | Funding | Diversification of study provision | Equity |
| Lifelong learning | Digitalization | Internationalization | Quality |

Source: Author's compilation.

The Gaps

However, there are a number of important gaps in data and information vis-à-vis the conceptual framework for benchmarking the performance of the education function of higher-education systems.

Learning Outcomes and Learning Gains

There are no internationally comparable data on the learning outcomes of higher-education graduates. The only available internationally comparable data is provided by the Survey of Adult Skills of the Programme for the International Assessment of Adult Competencies (PIAAC). However, this survey was not designed for measuring the learning outcomes of higher-education graduates. It is designed to measure skill levels of the general adult population. As such, it only provides information on generic literacy and numeracy proficiency, rather than specific graduate skills. In addition, for some countries the samples for graduates are quite small, and the survey is planned to be repeated only every ten years. Furthermore, there is no internationally comparable measure of learning gains, as there is no information on skills on entry to higher education for the graduates surveyed.

The OECD Assessment of Higher Education Learning Outcomes (AHELO) feasibility study established that a large-scale comparative assessment of higher-education learning outcomes is conceptually valid and for the most part technically feasible, but the project did not continue. The OECD is now working with the Council for Aid to Education (CAE) to explore the use of the CLA+ International as an alternative method to measure generic student-learning outcomes in higher education in a number of countries.

This is an area of continuing interest where further developments could change the current emphasis on the research performance of higher education to a more balanced approach that recognizes the importance of the teaching and learning performance.

Equity

There are few international comparable metrics on equity, although the situation has improved recently. The OECD Indicators of Education Systems (INES) program is developing new indicators on equity in tertiary education for publication in the OECD *Education at a Glance* series. The new indicators cover six variables: age, gender, parental education, immigrant background, students with dependent children, and students from rural provenance. Data is collected for new entrants and first-time graduates.

In terms of measuring equity of outcomes, more needs to be done to disaggregate the data by groups of interest for graduate outcomes. We expect further interest and development in this area.

Education activities

The activities stage of the performance model in Figure 7.1 is currently the black box of higher education. Little is known about the teaching and learning practices of higher education, especially in a comparable way to be used in a benchmarking exercise. The first benchmarking exercise undertaken in 2017–18 uses qualitative descriptions provided by countries regarding their policies and the relevant practices emerging from them.

In the future, information will need to be collected in a more structured and standardized way, helping to improve the analytical power of the benchmarking exercises. This could be achieved through international surveys of relevant actors in higher education, such as students, staff, graduates, and employers.

Sub-sectors of Higher Education

There are over 18,000 higher-education institutions that offer at least a postgraduate degree or a four-year professional diploma in 180 countries (International Association of Universities and UNESCO Information Centre on Higher Education 2016). Less than 10 percent of these institutions have at least fifty publications in the most comprehensive indexed database of publications (Bonaccorsi et al. 2017), and this tends to be the research-intensive university sub-sector of higher education. Most available metrics and qualitative data on the activities of higher education tend to focus on this sector, even though they often represent the minority share.

Although the OECD benchmarking project was conceived to cover the whole of higher education, a lack of data for the non-university sub-sector and the private independent sector makes achieving this objective more difficult. Again, this is an area where we expect to see some changes, as countries are increasingly interested in gaining a better understanding of the performance of their whole higher-education system.

Conclusion

Coates (2017) notes that "a casual participant [in higher education] cannot help but notice how things could be improved." He calls for more transparency in higher-education systems as a lever to change things for the better.

The benchmarking approach described above contributes to this debate by making the relative performance of each system in different dimensions more transparent. It complements traditional metric benchmarking with policy and practice benchmarking, by not only comparing metrics, but also by comparing policies, which allows for peer learning, spurring new ideas and policies, and driving creativity and innovation. Systems can use the information and the analysis to inform the design, implementation, and evaluation of policies, and thus continuously enhance the performance of higher-education systems.

Acknowledgements

The chapter has been informed by the OECD Enhancing Higher-Education System Performance project, which is being developed by the Higher-Education Team, Skills beyond Schools Division, Directorate for Education and Skills, under the auspices of the Informal Working Group on Higher Education of the Education Policy Committee. The opinions expressed in this article are those of the author and do not necessarily reflect the views of the OECD and of its members.

References

Barrie, Simon, Clair Hughes, Geoffrey Crisp, and Anne Bennison. 2014. *Assessing and Assuring Australian Graduate Learning Outcomes: Principles and Practices Within and Across Disciplines: Final Report 2014.* Sydney: Australian Government Office for Learning and Teaching.

Bonaccorsi, Andrea, Peter Haddawy, Tindaro Cicero, and Saeed-Ul Hassan. 2017. "The Solitude of Stars. An Analysis of the Distributed Excellence Model of European Universities." *Journal of Informetrics* 11 (2): 435–54.

Coates, Hamish. 2017. *The Market for Learning: Leading Transparent Higher Education.* Singapore: Springer.

European Commission. 2015. *Dropout and Completion in Higher Education in Europe.* Luxembourg: Publications Office of the European Union.

Eurydice. 2014. *Modernisation of Higher Education in Europe: Access, Retention and Employability 2014*. Luxembourg: Publications Office of the European Union.

Galindo-Rueda, Fernando, and Anna Vignoles. 2005. "The Declining Relative Importance of Ability in Predicting Educational Attainment." *The Journal of Human Resources* 40 (2): 335–53.

Goff, Lori, Michael K. Potter, Eleanor Pierre, Thomas Carey, Amy Gullage, Erika Kustra, Rebecca Lee, Valerie Lopes, Leslie Marshall, Lynn Martin, Jessica Raffoul, Abeer Siddqui, and Greg Van Gastel. 2015. *Learning Outcomes Assessment: A Practitioner's Handbook*. Toronto: Higher Education Quality Council of Ontario.

Hazelkorn, Ellen. 2015. *Rankings and the Reshaping of Higher Education: The Battle for World-Class Excellence*. 2nd ed. Basingstoke: Palgrave Macmillan.

———. 2017. *Rankings and Higher Education: Reframing Relationships Within and Between States*. London: Centre for Global Higher Education.

International Association of Universities and UNESCO Information Centre on Higher Education. 2016. *International Handbook of Universities 2017*. Basingstoke: Palgrave Macmillan.

Johnes, Jill, and Jim Taylor. 1990. *Performance Indicators in Higher Education*. Buckingham: SRHE and Open University Press.

Johnstone, D. Bruce, and Pamela N. Marcucci. 2007. *Worldwide Trends in Higher Education Finance: Cost-Sharing, Student Loans, and the Support of Academic Research*. UNESCO Forum on Higher Education, Research and Development.

McCormick, Alexander C., Jillian Kinzie, and Robert M. Gonyea. 2013. "Student Engagement: Bridging Research and Practice to Improve the Quality of Undergraduate Education." In *Higher Education: Handbook of Theory and Research: Volume 28*, edited by Michael B. Paulsen, 47–92. Dordrecht: Springer.

OECD (Organisation for Economic Co-operation and Development). 2017. *Benchmarking Higher Education System Performance: Conceptual Framework and Data, Enhancing Higher Education System Performance*. Paris: OECD Publishing.

Quinn, Jocey. 2013. *Drop-out and Completion in Higher Education in Europe Among Students from Under-Represented Groups*. Brussels: European Union.

Schleicher, Andreas. 2015. "Value-Added: How Do You Measure Whether Universities Are Delivering for Their Students?" 2015 HEPI

Annual Lecture, London, 1 December.

The Economist. 2017. "Higher Education and Wages: Which British Universities Do Most to Boost Graduate Salaries?" 12 August.

Wagenaar, Robert. 2018. "What Do We Know—What Should We Know? Measuring and Comparing Achievements of Learning in European Higher Education: Initiating the New CALOHEE Approach." In *Assessment of Learning Outcomes in Higher Education*, edited by Olga Zlatkin-Troitschanskaia, Miriam Toepper, Hans Anand Pant, Corinna Lautenbach, Christiane Kuhn. Wiesbaden: Springer (forthcoming).

Weingarten, Harvey P. 2014. "We Have to Measure Literacy and Numeracy among University Graduates." *The Globe and Mail*, 12 September.

Weingarten, Harvey P., Martin Hicks, Linda Jonker, Carrie Smith, and Hillary Arnold. 2015. *Canadian Postsecondary Performance: IMPACT 2015*. Toronto: Higher Education Quality Council of Ontario.

Section III

Canada

8

The Sweet Smell of Student Success: Demonstrating Learning Experience Quality in Ontario

Maureen Mancuso

Throughout modern history, there have always been concerns over a perceived decline in the quality of postsecondary teaching and the student learning experience. While to some extent this reflects a common perceptual bias (most experiences improve in memory over time), we can acknowledge that the pervasiveness of these concerns is itself an issue. There is a widespread feeling that "things are worse than they were," but little agreement about which things; different critics use different metrics in different ways.

Addressing these concerns—and responding to them with practical measures to enhance teaching and learning quality—will require a more comprehensive approach to measuring and demonstrating quality, but assessing something as complex and multifaceted as the learning experience is a difficult problem. It is hard to characterize quality in a systematic (reliable, repeatable) and meaningful (relevant, actionable) way. The learning experience also exposes many easy-to-measure variables that tempt stakeholders to cherry-pick and create superficially consistent (but internally incomplete) models, which in turn can undermine policy choices by introducing counterproductive incentives.

Meanwhile, universities and the university system have made excellent progress on encouraging and enhancing the research enterprise, in part by identifying systematic and meaningful metrics that assess and incentivize practices and policies that enhance research quality and output. But there is a growing sense that this emphasis has short-changed the teaching side of the university effort and the student learning experience that is so dependent on the quality of teaching and the commitment of the teachers. Some go so far as to suggest that universities have essentially abandoned their teaching mission in favour of pursuing research—and research funding (Clark et al. 2009).

I would argue that such a charge is unwarranted and exaggerated, but the fact that it seems plausible is a warning sign. The teaching mission is vital to the university model and a perceived imbalance between research and teaching is a contributing factor to the ongoing difficulty universities are experiencing in marshalling and sustaining public support. Moreover, in the absence of a clear and compelling way to demonstrate quality in the learning experience and in the context of ever-rising costs, concerns over the "value for money" or "return on investment" of a university education continue to be raised, along with suggestions that the current university model may be unsustainable.[1] This sort of narrative of decline has gained traction in some circles, even though it rests largely upon the perceptions (and policy preferences) of certain external stakeholders rather than systematic evidence of actual student performance.[2]

How, then, do we ensure that the student learning experience helps position students for success? How do we help students understand, document, and present the knowledge, skills, and values they have acquired through their university experience? How do we demonstrate to other stakeholders the full worth and quality of that experience?

Assessing research quality (and rewarding it appropriately) is not a trivial task but, today, the mechanisms we use to do so—metrics, processes, and policy levers—are still more deterministic, direct, and quantitative than the largely hortatory efforts made to promote enhanced teaching quality. Not surprisingly, institutions have responded to this clarity and invested in efforts to reap those more predictable rewards.

---

1 For a perspective on "return on investment" see Coates and Morrison (2013); Clark, Trick, and Van Loon (2011) make this argument about the current model.
2 The narrative also persists in the face of coarse-grained evidence supporting "value." For example, since 2008, despite having the lowest level of per-student funding in Canada, Ontario has some of the highest performance metric scores (Weingarten et al. 2015).

When teaching is assessed by flawed or incomplete metrics—either quantitative but oversimplified ones such as student-to-faculty ratios, or extremely subjective and inscrutable ones like reputation—it is hard to identify clear return on investment.

But the desire for a better, more accurate, more transparent measurement of teaching and learning quality cannot rest solely on transactional accountability to external stakeholders. To do so, fosters another misleading narrative that quality standards are something that must be imposed on universities from without, and that unless forced to do so by others, universities and colleges would neglect issues of quality and give only lackadaisical commitment to student success (Ikenberry and Kuh 2015). We need to acknowledge the genuine, sincere, and institutionally driven commitment to enhancing learning quality for its own sake: "Accountability for improving student learning as an enactment of the moral and professional commitments of faculty, staff and institutions rather than as a reaction to externally imposed obligations, is an idea that rarely surfaces in the public discourse about assessment and accountability" (Blaich and Wise 2011, 6).

Better, more accurate, more evidence-based and transparent measurements of teaching and learning quality would not only counter assertions of decline or neglect, which we as academics believe to be unjustified, but also refocus attention on the sometimes overlooked innovations being pursued organically. And part of that innovation ought to be reclaiming definitional leadership or at least a strong voice in just what quality means.

In October 2015, the Ontario Council of Academic Vice-Presidents (OCAV) formed the Task Force on Quality Indicators in the Undergraduate Learning Experience to address these issues. The task force had two complementary goals: to counter the popular narrative of decline with more compelling information about the genuine efforts undertaken by universities to maintain and enhance quality in the learning experience, and to do so by devising a more convincing, more authentic, more practically implementable scheme of measurement that could demonstrate and document that quality to both internal and external stakeholders.

The Task Force and its Approach

The task force's work was grounded in the context of Ontario's established quality assurance processes, which are organized around periodic self-assessment and peer review, overseen by a quality council that functions at arm's length from both the universities and the government. A set of undergraduate degree-level expectations (UDLEs) serve as academic standards and identify knowledge and skill outcomes and progression levels for the sector.[3] The task force also recognized the importance of skills and competencies in developing qualified individuals and a highly skilled workforce in Ontario, and supported the recommendations and directions set out in the Ontario government's 2016 highly skilled workforce report (Premier's Highly Skilled Workforce Expert Panel 2016).

But the task force was also determined to make good use of contemporary research on the question of learning-outcomes assessment, including the work done by the Association of American Colleges & Universities (AAC&U) and the National Institute for Learning Outcomes Assessment (NILOA), which has focused especially on course-embedded assessments as a more authentic way of measuring student learning. A recent AAC&U paper has documented that many institutions of higher education are, in fact, moving toward these types of assessments and away from standardized tests such as the Collegiate Learning Assessment's generic skills test, as these provide insufficient information to administrators and are often not taken seriously by students (Hart Research Associates 2016).

Our research and, indeed our experience, convinced us of the need for reliable, authentic, outcomes-based measures of quality. Establishing such a regime is not something that can be done overnight, but the current lack of fully developed metrics does not mean we cannot start building toward that goal, using currently feasible proxies where needed to stand in for more robust assessment metrics as they are developed and deployed. Experience elsewhere—not only in other jurisdictions, but also in professional programs within the province where these types of measures are already in place—suggests that doing so properly is a project best approached on an eight- to ten-year timeline, in part because the cycle of refining measurements and processes is rate-limited by the academic year, and also because effective learning-outcomes assessment requires substantial effort by faculty and staff at the course and curriculum levels.

The problem is by no means a dearth of data about quality. A great deal of relevant data is already collected by universities for administra-

---

3   See http://oucqa.ca/framework/appendix-1/ for details of the UDLEs.

tive processes or is required by government, although it is not necessarily readily available in the form of metrics. We need to acquire and model this information in more accessible and commensurable form, with clearer interpretive guidelines, and distill that raw data into more meaningful, actionable indicators and metrics of quality that can enable effective policy levers. There is much we can do now to begin developing improved performance indicators with the data we have while preparing for and enriching the data we collect in the future.

Defining and Selecting Performance Indicators

Performance indicators have been gaining currency among governments and postsecondary institutions in other jurisdictions (including Australia, the UK, and the United States) as a way to increase efficiency, quality, and accountability in higher education. And different jurisdictions have different performance models, reflecting, in part, different challenges. For example, in the US (in contrast with Ontario), low completion and graduation rates are a significant concern and, therefore, the indicator-driven funding levers have been primarily oriented to encourage attainment. In the UK, a key policy goal is to allow quality measurements to support differentiated tuition levels; indicator development there emphasizes classification and tiering of institutions by perceived quality of teaching and learning (For more on the Teaching Excellence Framework, see Chapter 4, Governance and Power Through Indicators: The UK Higher Education Teaching Excellence and Student Outcomes Framework). Australia has focused mostly on a variety of experience and satisfaction surveys, the results of which are published to assist students in making better institutional choices and as a means to improve retention, completion, and employability; some surveys are centrally mandated and others are oriented toward differentiated, per-institution priorities and goals.[4]

Although there is no common definition of performance indicators, according to Denise Chalmers they "cannot be considered 'facts' but are goal, value and context laden, and utilized in different ways depending on the performance model being employed" (Chalmers 2008, 9). In other words, performance indicators ought to be collected and used to facilitate benchmarking and institutional and sector self-reflection and self-improvement. With this in mind, it is important to recognize

---

4 See http://www.qilt.edu.au for examples of the evaluations.

that quantitative (input and output) indicators, while generally easy to gather, illuminate only part of the overall picture. Inputs and outputs treat the system being measured—the learning experience—as a simple "black box" and, therefore, provide limited insight into how that system works, and little to no insight into how it might be improved. The common criticism of "throwing money at the problem" is an explicit recognition that trying to force outputs (such as graduation rates) to improve by simply driving up inputs (such as funding) is acknowledged to be an unviable approach.

Qualitative indicators, while more difficult to collect and interpret, can be more meaningful in measuring teaching and learning quality, and capturing information that can be used to facilitate improvement. Quantitative indicators are often simpler to explain and more objective in and of themselves, but interpreting what they actually mean in terms of effect on quality is more subjective and contentious. Qualitative indicators may be more complex in definition, but they can often better capture the nuances of learning as it is experienced by students—in different ways by different individuals—instead of treating it as a homogenous aggregate (Hamshire et al. 2017). Both types of indicators are needed to paint a clear and accurate picture.

The two main categories of qualitative indicators are outcomes and processes. Outputs only tell us about delivery: "What (or how much) was done?" Outcome indicators tell us about impact: "What difference did it make?" Process indicators tell us about the integrity of the learning experience: "How (and why) were the inputs utilized, outputs delivered, and outcomes achieved?" Process indicators are especially important as they directly reflect the network of policies and procedures put in place—at all scales: course, unit, institution, and system—to enhance and assure quality of the learning experience. Taken together, outcome and process indicators can balance and supplement the coarse-grained picture offered by qualitative inputs and outputs and sharpen the focus on quality.

In selecting indicators, we also considered other attributes that impact their practical utility. Volatility is the extent to which an indicator tends to fluctuate over time for reasons outside institutional control, or as a function of the data. Volatile indicators introduce additional complications into their interpretation and require additional baselining and calibration, but they are often unavoidable when tracking data that is subject to inherent long-term trends, such as demographics. Examples include small-to-medium sample size surveys and employment outcomes. Specificity describes the degree to which accountabilities can be assigned within an institution for performance. Highly specific indicators can provide significant policy leverage through clear lines of responsibility, but can also tend to be overly narrow in focus. Capability is the extent to which an institution as a whole can affect performance or move the needle on an indicator and thus be held accountable for changes. And, obviously, availability—current or future—plays into indicator selection. Indicators that cannot be deployed are of little use, but as a metric framework is rolled out, we want to identify where currently available metrics that might have some drawbacks can be used as a bridge to more robust and reliable measurement processes in the future.

In the end, there are far more measurements that can be taken—and at least partially justified as relevant and useful—than can be effectively deployed in a manageable process. The core problem is less about identifying viable indicators and more about organizing a suite of indicators to achieve appropriate breadth of coverage in a tractable size. The learning experience is complex and multi-faceted: Which aspects of it are most important to capture in a compact suite of indicators? How do we structure and balance that suite to maintain appropriate representation of those aspects? Because indicators in an assessment framework naturally give rise to organizational incentives at the policy level, how do we ensure that the emphasis of the suite promotes positive change? Institutional differentiation and autonomy means that different choices will be needed and made in different contexts: How do we ensure that these harmonize across the system in a way that respects variation without fragmentation? How do we guide institutions to make compatible choices?

The task force considered a number of ways to try to organize and balance indicator selection. In the end, we settled on a scheme with three primary axes of variation: one focusing on the phase of the student life cycle that the indicator examines (when), another reflecting the availability and generality of the indicator for measurement by institutions (how), and the third classifying the indicator with respect to certain prioritized aspects of the learning experience (which).

When: The Student Life Cycle

An authentic assessment of quality has to include the entire student learning experience, from start to finish. And we know that the transitions into and out of university are especially critical phases of that experience. We therefore divided the life cycle into three stages:

- Getting There: The incoming transition covers areas like student recruitment, application processes, admissions, accessibility, and the many intellectual and personal challenges associated with the shift from secondary to postsecondary levels of instruction and personal responsibility. Indicators for this phase are especially important for helping students and their families make informed institutional choices.
- Being There: The core cycle of student life between matriculation and graduation covers areas like program delivery, student services, retention, advising and program guidance, and student engagement. Indicators for this phase illuminate enriching experiences both in and out of the classroom and can help students pursue and refine their goals as the university experience reveals to them new areas of potential interest and intellectual possibility.
- Leaving There: the outgoing transition, covers areas like culminating and capstone experiences, graduation and post-graduate access, career planning and placement, student satisfaction, learning outcomes, and degree valuation. These indicators help position students for continued success by making their degrees less opaque, and help them understand and demonstrate to employers and others the knowledge, skills, and values they have acquired in their program of study.

This simple, sequential model isn't intended as a universal template for the experiences of actual students, many of whom will take a more elaborate path from matriculation to graduation (for example, "being there" is non-contiguous time for an increasing number of students, both traditional and mature). Instead, this student life cycle model should be seen as just an organizational tool, a way of tagging candidate indicators with the phase or phases they address, to highlight whether an indicator suite is appropriately balanced and reflective of the whole experience. It separates the distinct challenges that are important in each phase and also acknowledges linkages; some outputs or outcomes from one phase naturally serve as inputs for the processes of following phases.

How: Indicator Availability and Generality

In a workable quality-assessment scheme there will need to be some indicators that all institutions report. A system framework needs some system-wide universality in order to satisfy government requirements for accountability and to facilitate identification of effective practices. But the richness of educational quality in a diverse system cannot be adequately captured by fully standardized metrics alone because the Ontario system—by design—affords individual institutions the autonomy to pursue differentiated missions and priorities within an envelope of overall core standards and expectations. There are important aspects of learning experience quality—and thus meaningful and valuable indicators—that apply with different emphasis or priority at different institutions.

Because of this, the second organizational axis chosen by the task force reflects the methodology and availability of indicators. Universal, standard indicators are those that can be gathered and reported on by all institutions in a uniform way. Many of these we already collect and provide as part of the Strategic Mandate Agreement (SMA) and the predecessor Multi-Year Accountability Agreement (MYAA) processes or as required by the Ministry of Advanced Education and Skills Development (MAESD) and reflect government priorities (such as access and success for under-represented groups, experiential learning, and student mobility and credit transfer). These indicators serve especially to identify where an institution fits in the context of the overall system and what it emphasizes within the common goals that all institutions serve.

Universal, non-standard indicators are those that can be provided by all institutions, but the methodology used might vary according to institution-specific practice or analytical tools, and the results would not be directly commensurable. This category acknowledges that not all quality metrics can or should be measured in precisely the same way in a diverse system.

Discretionary indicators are those that would be chosen by individual institutions to focus on specific aspects of quality that have important local relevance, and would serve the important purpose of identifying and emphasizing what makes an institution special or unique. This class of indicator highlights the non-systemic goals and priorities each institution has chosen to pursue (and in doing so, how it has extended the breadth and depth of the system as a whole) and thereby furthers the overall government goal of promoting enhanced differentiation.

Which: Aspects of Quality

"When" and "how" are purely organizational dimensions; ways to categorize indicators and balance their coverage. The notion of "which" kinds of indicators to focus on introduces a preference and an emphasis that is necessarily reflective of subjective values and priorities and represents an opinion about what parts of the learning experience are most crucial and have the most impact on overall quality. The other axes of classification allow us to assign a category to any indicator based on its target or methodology; the "which" axis is instead meant to assign to only some possible indicators a special distinction or marker, a star denoting extra merit and desirability in a well-considered suite. There is nothing wrong with choosing indicators that do not fit into one of these aspects of emphasis, but they should trigger additional questions about why they are more appropriate for the institution and the system than an alternative.

In deciding which aspects of quality to designate for special attention, the task force once again considered the literature on quality assessment, but also acknowledged that a practical framework must also satisfy the priorities of key stakeholders who have their own ideas about what constitutes quality and what needs to be maximized. The government had already identified a number of priorities in its quality initiatives, including access, a shift from an enrolment-based funding model to one that is outcomes-based, and an emphasis on job-ready skills and work-integrated and experiential learning. After considering these areas and many other existing and potential metrics, the task force chose to recommend that special emphasis be given to indicators that fall into four thematic clusters: diversity and access; engagement and student support; learning outcomes, results, and student success; and high-impact practices.

- Diversity and access indicators (such as proportional participation by under-represented groups) acknowledge and respect the province's commitment to ensure that participation in postsecondary education is available to all qualified and committed students, and the principle that a diverse learning environment is a rich, rewarding, and ultimately more effective one.
- Engagement and student support indicators (such as the National Survey of Student Engagement) address the proven advantages of

actively engaged learning, both inside and outside the classroom, and the services and practices that support student learning.

- Learning outcomes, results, and success indicators help students demonstrate what they have learned and document the real-world value of their educational experience, and the knowledge, skills, and values they have acquired in a compelling and authentic manner. Populating this category of indicators requires extended investment in an outcomes focus, which is still ongoing, but we can develop initial metrics to serve as a bridging strategy while outcomes measurement and infrastructure are built up over time.
- Indicators for High-Impact Practices (HIPs) focus on well-defined learning practices that have been repeatedly and compellingly shown to be associated with especially effective learning: service/community learning, first-year seminars, learning communities, research experiences, semesters abroad, capstone projects, writing-intensive courses, internships, global learning, and collaborative assignments and projects (Kuh 2008). Many of these practices qualify as experiential learning (as long as that term is not too narrowly defined as strictly workplace-based activities). HIPs exercise and develop in a wider set of contexts and environments many of the same skills attributed to work-integrated learning. This list of HIPs is not static: the common link among them is that they are active and engaged learning practices that create lasting impacts on skill-acquisition, including critical thinking, oral and written communication, teamwork, collaboration, and problem solving.

This HIPs cluster is admittedly related to, and overlaps with, the other three, but the task force felt that it represents a particularly important facet of quality that deserves to be singled out for special attention. Moreover, the utility and impact of HIPs is well established in the literature, and there are concrete examples in multiple other jurisdictions of how they can be successfully deployed and measured (Kuh, O'Donnell, and Reed 2013). HIPs have been shown to deliver significant gains in student success of the very type that all parties have sought, in particular many of the perceived skills and experiences associated with work-integrated learning, but more broadly.

The Framework in Practice

This organizational framework evolved as the task force considered a wide variety of potential indicators and we prepared several iterations of a map that assigned indicators (and areas of potential indicator development) to the various categories. This mapping exercise helped guide the choice of the thematic clusters as we began to get a sense of what metrics seemed to be particularly salient when viewed from the framework's perspective. The task force proposed to OCAV that all universities report on a small number of universal indicators (standard and non-standard). Each university would also supplement this common set with additional discretionary indicators they deemed especially relevant to their institutional mission and priorities. We also proposed that each graduating student should have the opportunity to participate in at least two HIPs. This proposal was strongly supported by OCAV and the task force then set out to identify specific, concrete, universal metrics for the sector.

Meanwhile, Back at Queen's Park

Throughout all of its deliberations, the task force remained engaged with MAESD officials and both groups recognized that they were addressing overlapping issues, even if the task force had the luxury of a far narrower focus (and only in an advisory capacity). We did not formally coordinate our work with the Ministry, but over the course of periodic meetings it became clear that our approach—and the framework we devised—was garnering attention and recognition within the MAESD as something quite compatible with its broader goals. It was eventually signalled that if the task force could obtain OCAV institutional consensus on a deployable indicator scheme, the Ministry would consider it as part of its overall strategy. The catch was that the Ministry also wanted to be able to deploy those indicators at the outset of round two of the Strategic Management Agreement process (2017–18).

We were thus, to some extent, victims of our own success and were left with an accelerated schedule and less time to develop and refine our initial indicator suite. On the other hand, we had always intended for the indicators to evolve significantly over time from a pragmatic first draft and the added time pressure, in a sense, made it easier to bypass premature optimization discussions. And by obtaining support from the MAESD, this project represented a visible instance of the sector and its institutions being out in front rather than playing catch-up to governmental priorities and directives.

Moreover, because of the short turnaround time, we were able to secure some basic guarantees about the use of the indicator framework. In particular, while the availability of universal standard indicators makes it inherently possible to compare institutions, such indicators will not be used to create a zero-sum resource competition within the sector, where indicator performance would dictate the relative allocation of a fixed pie. Rather, institutions will compete only against their own stated goals (as articulated in their SMAs); and indicators will be used to assess institutional performance against a pre-allocated envelope.[5] The risk in any system that attempts to reduce a vast and complex process like the learning experience to a small set of numbers is the emergence of perverse incentives to game the system rather than to put effort into real, distinct achievement. When all players are chasing the same reward, the kind of creative differentiation the government wants for the sector is discouraged, in favour of mimicry and me-too-ism.

Implementing the task force's framework as part of round two of the SMAs required adapting it to the overall strategy devised by the Ministry, which identified five broad priority themes: the student experience; innovation in teaching and learning; access and equity; research excellence and impact; and innovation, economic development, and community engagement. Our work on quality assessment was a good fit with the first two categories and part of the third. After reviewing the structure of our indicator proposal (a mix of system-wide universal indicators with per-institution discretionary ones), the MAESD adopted it as an organizational principle for the other two categories as well (and the Ontario Council on University Research developed a corresponding proposal for research-related indicators). Institutions are expected to negotiate overall weightings for each of the five themes along with appropriate discretionary indicators.

After working to adapt its candidate metrics to fit within the Ministry's themes, the task force ultimately proposed the following set of indicators:

---

5 The eventual intent is that some of the funding envelope will be distributed contingent on meeting the negotiated performance targets; initially (during round two of the SMAs as the new formula is rolled out), the targets will be advisory and will not directly impact funding levels.

The Student Experience

- Proportion of fourth-year students participating in at least two High Impact Practices: All universities participate in the National Survey of Student Engagement, so this data is readily available.[6]
- Year one to year two retention percentage: This metric is already gathered and reported to the Ministry and is a useful probe of the larger transition from "getting there" to "being there."[7]
- Student services expenses as a proportion of overall expenses (net of financial support): A quantitative input indicator that attempts to approximate the investment campuses make in creating a supportive learning environment for their students. This would include a range of services like program advising, career counselling, peer support programs, Learning Commons, writing services, personal counselling, and a plethora of other services that contribute to a high-quality student experience. This figure is already reported in the *Maclean's* survey.

Innovation in Teaching and Learning

- Composite scores on NSSE questions related to perceived gains in learning outcomes: This includes skills like critical thinking, written and oral clarity of expression and effectiveness, numeracy, working effectively with others, and problem solving; institutions would all report on this measure. While it is acknowledged that these are student self-reported gains, research supports that these student perceptions are not far off from actual reported gains that have been assessed and measured (Douglass, Thomson and Zhao 2012).
- Proportion of programs with explicit curricular maps and articulated learning outcomes: Curricular maps are helpful guideposts for students in identifying paths through their program. The map

---

6 This indicator could have alternatively been located in the Innovation in Teaching and Learning domain, given that most of the HIPs rely on innovative pedagogies and have been proven to result in effective learning. But in a practical effort to balance the indicators we had, and in recognition of the contribution these value-added practices have to the overall student experience, we chose to place it in this category.

7 The difference between the KPI (key performance indicators) reported to government and the retention metric the task force adopted is that we are using data from the Consortium for Student Retention Data Exchange (CSRDE) which is based on first-entry programs only.

will also indicate what knowledge, skills, and values particular courses contribute to their overall educational experience and should help to position students to speak compellingly about what they have learned and are able to do upon the completion of the program.

- Graduation rate: A straightforward quantitative output that is widely used as a bellwether, and also for cross-system comparisons (although not without methodological risk due to differences in context). Completion rates are commonly employed in all jurisdictions that have a focus on outcomes and are widely regarded as a standard indicator of student success.

Access and Equity

- Enrolment of under-represented groups, including Indigenous students, francophone students, first-generation students, and students with disabilities. These figures are also already gathered and reported using a variety of collection methods (and thus represent universal non-standard metrics).

This initial proposal was a compromise between short-term feasibility and longer-term plans. The framework as a whole expresses what we think could be done with sustained effort and investment, but we felt it would be best to exploit familiar processes at first in order to encourage acceptance and adoption of the overall approach.

Just as the task force intentionally took a first-draft approach to an indicator framework, the MAESD is positioning this scheme as a first step toward a more developed outcomes-based grant funding formula, and the use of the SMA as an accountability mechanism. There is still a possibility that a more directly competitive environment might be created in the future, but we are hopeful that continued research showing unintended consequences and inequitable repercussions from such systems elsewhere will be convincing (Dougherty et al. 2016). The reality is that false narratives—whether about a decline in quality or the resistance of universities to self-improvement without outside pressure—are difficult to stamp out, and need continuous counterargument.

Conclusions and Next Steps

With the second round of SMAs set to be signed off by fall 2017, the task force is continuing its work to refine and evolve the indicator suite, and the underlying organization/selection framework, with an eye to the next round of SMA negotiations due to begin in 2020. A key goal going forward is to gather feedback from the sector, stakeholders, students, and faculty to help ensure that our deployed metrics are relevant, appropriate, and meaningful, and to allow them to evolve in the right direction. We also want to support and initiate pilot projects in new forms of authentic assessment, and consider the development of a system of course-tagging for HIPs and experiential learning. There are a host of technical issues to digest and discuss, remaining definitional issues to be resolved, and a more effective data strategy and implementation tools to be developed. We will continue to stay productively engaged with the Ministry on tactics, strategy, and approach.

We remain committed to marshalling evidence to support the narrative that we want to tell: that our institutions, our faculty, and staff are dedicated to the success of our students. Defining and devising a set of indicators that satisfies the needs and expectations of—or, at least in its initial form, is acceptable to—the varied and sometimes opposed constituencies involved in assessing educational quality has been a difficult but rewarding effort, a first step in a journey that will ideally become easier now that some momentum has been established. We must continue to foster an environment of innovation and experimentation because quality is not a static target. And we need to ensure that we equip our students with the appropriate information and language to describe and communicate the knowledge, skills, and values they have acquired during their time with us. What must be kept in mind is that the ultimate purpose of this effort is not simply to satisfy stakeholders, but to use these metrics and indicators to drive genuine improvement and have an impact on the experiences of our students.

Acknowledgement

The author serves as the chair of the Council of Ontario Universities Task Force on Quality Indicators. This chapter and the accomplishments described are the work of all members of the group.

References

Blaich, Charles, and Kathleen Wise. 2011. "From Gathering to Using Assessment Results: Lessons from the Wabash National Study." *NILOA Occasional Paper*, No. 8 (Jan).

Chalmers, Denise. 2008. *Indicators of University Teaching and Learn-*

ing Quality. Australian Learning & Teaching Council. https://www.re searchgate.net/publication/265248222_INDICATORS_OF_UNIVERSI TY_TEACHING_AND_LEARNING_QUALITY

Clark, Ian D., David Trick, and Richard Van Loon. 2011. *Academic Reform: Policy Options for Improving the Quality and Cost-Effectiveness of Undergraduate Education in Ontario.* Montreal and Kingston: Mc-Gill-Queens University Press.

Clark, Ian D., Greg Moran, Michael Skolink, and David Trick. 2009. *Academic Transformation: The Forces Reshaping Higher Education.* Montreal and Kingston: McGill-Queens University Press.

Coates, Ken S. and Bill Morrison. 2013. *Campus Confidential* (2nd ed). Toronto: James Lorimer and Company Ltd.

Dougherty, Kevin J., Sosanya, M. Jones, Hana Lahr, Rebecca S. Natow, Lara Pheatt, and Vikash Reddy. 2016. *Performance Funding for Higher Education.* Baltimore: Johns Hopkins University Press.

Douglass, John Aubrey, Gregg Thomson, and Chun Mei Zhao. 2012. "The Learning Outcomes Race: The Value of Self-reported Gains in Large Research Universities." *Higher Education: The International Journal of Higher Education and Educational Planning* 4 (3): 317–335. https://doi.org/10.1007/s10734-011-9496-x

Hamshire, Claire, Rachel Forsyth, Amani Bell, Matthew Benton, Roisin Kelly-Laubscher, Moragh Paxton, and 'Ema Wolfgramm-Foliaki. 2017. "The Potential of Student Narratives to Enhance Quality in Higher Education." *Quality in Higher Education* 23 (1): 50–64. http://dx.doi.org/10.1080/13538322.2017.1294407

Hart Research Associates. 2016. "Trends in Learning Outcomes Assessment: Key Findings from a Survey Among Administrators at AAC&U Member Institutions." Washington, DC: Hart Research Associates & AAC&U. https://www.aacu.org/sites/default/files/files/LEAP/2015_Survey_Report3.pdf

Ikenberry, Stanley O., and George D. Kuh. 2015. "From Compliance to Ownership; Why and How Colleges and Universities Assess Student Learning." In *Using Evidence of Student Learning to Improve Higher Education,* edited by George D. Kuh, Stanely O. Ikenberry, Natasha A. Jankowski, Timothy Reese Cain, Peter T. Ewell, Pat Hutchings, and Jillian Kinzie, 31–34 Hoboken: Jossey Bass.

Kuh, George D. 2008. *High Impact Practices: What They Are, Who Has Access to Them, and Why They Matter.* Washington, DC: American Association of Colleges and Universities.

Kuh, George D., Ken O'Donnell, and Sally Reed. 2013. *Ensuring Quality and Taking High Impact Practices to Scale*. Washington, DC: American Association of Colleges and Universities.

Premier's Highly Skilled Workforce Expert Panel. 2016. "Building the Workforce of Tomorrow: A Shared Responsibility." Toronto: Government of Ontario. https://www.ontario.ca/page/building-work-force-tomorrow-shared-responsibility

Weingarten, Harvey P., Martin Hicks, Linda Jonker, Carrie Smith, and Hillary Arnold. 2015. "Canadian Postsecondary Performance: Impact 2015." HEQCO, Toronto. http://www.heqco.ca/SiteCollectionDocuments/HEQCO_Canadian_Postsecondary_Performance_Impact2015.pdf

9

Supporting Quality Through Collaboration and Funding-Based Policy Levers: Nova Scotia's Experience

Duff Montgomerie, Ava Czapalay, and Jeremy Smith

Nova Scotia views its ten universities as important assets; they are important partners in helping Nova Scotia to advance its economic prosperity agenda. The universities collectively enrol 43,268 students (MPHEC 2017), and have long histories of attracting students from across Canada and from more than 120 countries around the world. The universities are magnets for retaining young Nova Scotians, and portals for welcoming people from all cultures to work, study, and live in Nova Scotia. Increasingly, prospective investors are meeting with universities to establish relationships, and to assess the potential for engaging with researchers, faculty, and students to access the talent needed to sustain their enterprises. It is, on the surface, a win-win situation.

The fundamental challenge, however, is that universities have not traditionally existed as suppliers of talent. Producing job-ready graduates may be the fortuitous by-product of their basic purpose of promoting knowledge, critical thinking, and understanding. Historically, "the idea that the university had any corporate interests that superseded those of the disciplines at an intellectual level was simply a non-starter: disciplinary interests would remain supreme. As far as academics were concerned that was—and is—the deal" (Usher 2014).

Today's reality is that students, families, and taxpayers are increasing

Assessing Quality in Postsecondary Education: International Perspectives, edited by Harvey P. Weingarten, Martin Hicks, and Amy Kaufman. Montréal and Kingston: McGill-Queen's University Press, Queen's Policy Studies Series. © 2018 The School of Policy Studies, Queen's University at Kingston. All rights reserved.

their investment in postsecondary education. As the public's financial stake in postsecondary education increases, it demands assurances, from government and from universities, that the investment of public money supports a quality experience that will generate future employment opportunities, and better prepare graduates for successful futures. Increasingly, universities and governments are pressured by students and industry to prepare job-ready graduates who are both educated in the traditional sense, while also trained with specific skills that will add value to a workplace. Success in connecting students with jobs is seen by the public as being linked to a quality education. The challenge, therefore, is how to provide supports and opportunities beyond the classroom that layer on practical skills while also ensuring that education for education's sake is not overlooked. Nova Scotia has chosen to focus on promoting collaborative activities that enhance the overall experience for students, and measuring the impact of students' experiences through a comprehensive survey managed through the Maritime Provinces Higher Education Commission (MPHEC).

In 2016–17, assistance to universities accounted for 3.75 percent, or $380.6 million, of the total provincial budget in Nova Scotia. This was the single largest investment of taxpayer dollars after healthcare, elementary and secondary education, community services, debt-servicing costs, and transportation and infrastructure renewal. Nova Scotians are aware of the investment they are making in postsecondary education, and a series of public consultations on the future of postsecondary education in Nova Scotia in 2014–15 revealed that stakeholders—taxpayers and students—believed there needed to be more accountability for how universities spend tuition and taxpayer dollars. "The overall purpose of the consultations was to solicit broad input and ideas from Nova Scotians; members of the business and international communities; university faculty, administration and students; and other stakeholders on the future of the postsecondary education system" (Halifax Global 2015, i). Twenty-nine consultation sessions with 240 stakeholders were held over a period of four months. "There is considerable recognition by stakeholders that our universities constitute assets that other jurisdictions would be pleased to have available; but at the same time, there is equal recognition that these assets are not being managed in a way that maximizes potential returns to stakeholders, including taxpayers" (Halifax Global 2015, ii).

When asked about the specific features of a quality university program, the stakeholders responded with an extensive list that included small class sizes, low faculty-to-student ratios, the overall quality of faculty as evidenced by teaching and research awards and publications, the availability and use of technology in classrooms and laboratories, and the ability to customize programs. Stakeholders indicated that co-op education, experiential learning, service learning, and opportunities to connect with local communities added value to their academic experience. Culturally diverse classrooms, campus life, and robust student services were identified as adding value to the students' experiences. In addition, participants in the consultations also agreed that universities need to find ways to be more cost effective and to link funding received from students and taxpayers to clearly defined outcomes (Halifax Global 2015).

The findings of the 2014–15 consultation were consistent with the results of a survey undertaken by the Times Higher Education Rankings on *Students' Indicators of Quality* (Times Higher Education 2017). In 2017, 15,000 UK students were interviewed about the quality of their university experience while attending universities in the UK. Like their Nova Scotia counterparts, the UK students referenced campus facilities, campus life, atmosphere, services, strong teaching, and opportunities to develop industry-relevant skills as key to a quality experience. The Nova Scotia consultation outcomes, reinforced by similar results in the Times Higher Education survey, indicate that students tend to bundle the quality of their academic experience with their entire university experience when reporting on their overall levels of satisfaction.

Nova Scotia's position is that academic quality is a component of the overall quality of experience that students, taxpayers, and employers expect from universities. This position is reflected in the 2015–19 Memorandum of Understanding (MOU) with the universities that includes a section on academic quality along with sections on tuition and fees, accessibility, improved supports for student success, and collaborative efforts to strengthen entrepreneurship, experiential learning, recruitment and retention, technology-enabled learning, and support for research and development.

During preparation of the MOU, the vice-presidents academic of the ten universities were asked to consider and agree upon fundamental measures of academic quality. Based upon their report, the MOU includes four key performance indicators (KPIs) in the section on "Educational Quality and Measures." The KPIs were developed with due consideration given to identifying measures that were practical; measures that institutions had the ability to track and report on progress.

A Program Quality Assurance KPI was developed that consists of four metrics relating to timely adherence to the existing program review process including institutional responsiveness to recommendations coming out of the reviews. The other three KPIs relate to measuring students' quality of experience and include "student satisfaction with educational experience; student experience post-graduation; and student progress within the Nova Scotia postsecondary education system." (Government of Nova Scotia 2016, 6).

The Program Quality Assurance KPI is supported by Nova Scotia's partnership in the MPHEC, which provides a program assessment service for Nova Scotia, New Brunswick, and Prince Edward Island universities that is supported by the three member provinces. The MPHEC validates institutional quality assurance frameworks against agreed-upon regional standards and undertakes ongoing quality assurance monitoring that involves the universities undertaking cyclical internal and external reviews and reporting back to the MPHEC. Nova Scotia ensures compliance through dialogue and collaboration; where best efforts are not successful, the province reserves the right to de-designate programs that are not compliant (de-designation means that students are not able to use student loans provided by the provincial and federal governments to pay for enrolment in such programs). It has been Nova Scotia's experience that the universities do not want to risk having a program de-designated, and that they work hard to ensure compliance.

The MPHEC also undertakes work that supports the MOU's three KPIs related to measuring students' quality of experience. Student satisfaction, student experience post-graduation, and student progress within the Nova Scotia postsecondary education system are monitored through the MPHEC's Measures of Student Progress and Outcomes work and the Graduate Outcomes Survey program. In its measures of student progress, the MPHEC considers university participation, persistence and graduation, time-to-degree, course success and failure, and graduation outcomes including employment. In addition, the MPHEC surveys Maritime university graduates on themes relating to workforce transition, earnings, student debt and repayment, retention and migration of new graduates, satisfaction with their degree post-graduation, and occupation and the relationship between work and education. These surveys are extensive, and provide universities and the provincial governments with useful data and analyses, including trends. The MPHEC's current survey focuses on graduates with bachelor's degrees from the 2012 and 2014 cohorts; the six-year cycle includes interviews two years after graduation and one cohort will be also interviewed in 2018, six years after graduation.

The reports emerging from these surveys provide important information to policy makers along with a comparative snapshot of performance within the region. The class of 2012 survey, for example, resulted in an MPHEC report entitled *Are University Graduates Satisfied with Their Education?* The report indicated that 95 percent of graduates surveyed were satisfied with their class sizes, 94 percent were satisfied with the availability of their professors, 93 percent were satisfied with the overall quality of education, and 92 percent were satisfied with the quality of teaching. The same study looked at student borrowing and found that the more money graduates had borrowed to finance their education, the less likely they were to report that the time and money invested was well worth it. (MPHEC 2015).

As required through the 2015 Universities Accountability and Sustainability Act, and in order to support the objectives of the 2015–19 MOU, Nova Scotia introduced outcome agreements in 2016–17. The outcome agreements replaced individual bilateral agreements and are much more structured. The agreements consist of two sections: Required Outcomes, which are centred on the themes of sustainable institutions and quality experience, and Institution-specific Outcomes, which allow institutions to select an additional two to five outcomes that are important to their mandate. Each institution also identified measures and metrics to track progress. Achievement of the outcomes will be directly linked to a percentage of operating grant funding beginning in 2018–19.

The required outcomes were identified and agreed upon through discussions at the partnership table, and bilateral discussions with each university, and through various high-level working groups. The agreed-upon shared priorities include:

- A sustainable, high-quality university system
- A focus on students
- A shared priority of growing Nova Scotia's prosperity, cultural development, and social well-being
- A commitment to collaboration and shared services

The province and the universities formed an innovation team that has worked to develop and implement programs and policies that would support the collective achievement of the shared priorities. Through the innovation team, the government and universities have looked at ways to improve overall quality of the student experience. Five key areas were identified: research, development, and innovation; entrepreneurship; experiential learning; technology-enabled learning; and student recruitment and retention. An innovation fund was created, and the universities developed and submitted collaborative proposals intended to significantly advance efforts to achieve quality outcomes in the five areas.

At the same time, the province approved a number of financial supports intended to assist the universities in maintaining a quality experience and achieving long-term sustainability. The province carried through on a promise to provide long-term funding to the universities, embedding in the 2015–19 MOU a 1 percent increase each year for four years. And finally, the province took measures to relieve financial pressure on the universities by allowing a one-time tuition reset to enable universities to increase tuition to levels similar to comparable programs in Canada and also to remove the tuition cap on graduate programs, and on tuition paid by students from out of province (the universities have, to date, chosen not to employ this final option).

The government introduced a graduate scholarship program and, importantly, allowed the universities to determine how best to structure the program with the caveat that it needed to spur graduate research in areas important to the provincial economy. Sandboxes were created on university campuses that have led to a sector-wide effort to enhance entrepreneurial skills and thinking. Almost 25 percent of the university student population participates in sandbox activities four years after they were established. And finally, in 2017, Nova Scotia created a $25 million trust that supports research activity on university campuses. Opportunities for students and new graduates to gain valuable research experience will expand as a result.

The MOU, the innovation team activities, and the outcome agreements are all intended to be "funding-based policy levers" (OECD 2016, 4), levers that link achievement of outcomes aligned with quality to increased operating funding. It is through collaboration and these policy levers that Nova Scotia has taken steps to ensure the quality university experience that students and the public expect.

Interestingly, the emphasis on providing a quality experience for all students has opened the doors to an enhanced academic experience. Collaboration, opportunity, and consumer demand are putting pressure on the traditional classroom lecture model. As one Nova Scotia president noted recently, universities are moving away from the "sage-on-the-stage" approach to something better described as a "guide-on-the-side" format. This shift is best illustrated with a few examples.

In recent years, and following the introduction of the sandbox pilot project that embedded collaborative, early-stage idea development spaces within several universities, Nova Scotia universities have increasingly incorporated entrepreneurship development into programming across curricula. We have, for example, a shared sandbox between Dalhousie University and the Nova Scotia College of Art and Design (NSCAD) that offers students credit courses to develop ideas with commercial potential. Student teams comprise design students from NSCAD and business and engineering students from Dalhousie, and are supported by faculty from both institutions. The sandbox environment is electric with both students and faculty fully engaged in learning. We also see more undergraduate students engaging in faculty research, helping to author academic articles, but also connecting their research to private industry needs.

And we are seeing more blending of academic and practical programming at the undergraduate level. Recently, Dalhousie University and the Nova Scotia Community College (NSCC) announced a formal "2+2 program" for students in management programs, which allows graduates with a two-year NSCC diploma to gain credit for up to two years of a four-year university degree. While not particularly surprising news, the announcement served to highlight the close relationship between the thirteen-campus college and the ten universities. The president of the NSCC is now invited to the table of the Council of Nova Scotia University Presidents. We expect that this collaboration will lead to further program customization and adaptation while improving the quality of the academic experience for students. Along with the breaking down of traditional barriers, the physical structure of universities is changing as well—research institutes, sandboxes, faculty offices, classroom spaces, and learning commons often share space on university campuses.

While it is too early to assess quantitative changes to the academic experience, the qualitative evidence is compelling: the experiences of Nova Scotia's university students are being enhanced through new and collaborative ways of engaging with faculty and students from other academic programs. We are hopeful that this new dynamic will improve the overall positive experience, while developing skills that lead to smart, curious, and engaged graduates—the kind of graduates that Nova Scotia's workforce wants and needs.

References

Government of Nova Scotia. 2016. *The Memorandum of Understanding between the Province of Nova Scotia and the Nova Scotia Universities (2015–2019)*. https://novascotia.ca/lae/pubs/docs/MOU-2015-2019.pdf

Halifax Global Inc. 2015. University System Visioning Consultations: Final Report. Halifax: Department of Labour and Advanced Education. 20 March. (http://novascotia.ca/lae/pubs/docs/HigherEducationVisioningReport.pdf)

MPHEC (Maritime Provinces Higher Education Commission). 2015. *Are University Graduates Satisfied with Their Education?* September. http://www.mphec.ca/media/111799/UniversityExperience_satisfaction_and_Statistical_Tables.pdf

———. 2017. *Trends in Maritime Higher Education,* Annual Digest 2015–2016. http://www.mphec.ca/media/142891/Annual-Digest-2015-2016.pdf

OECD (Organisation for Economic Co-operation and Development). 2016. *In-depth Analysis of the Labour Market Relevance and Outcomes of Higher Education Systems: Analytical Framework and Country Practices Report.* Directorate for Education and Skills, Enhancing Higher Education System Performance. Paris: OECD. 2 December.

Times Higher Education. 2017. "Student Experience Survey Results." 23 March. https://www.timeshighereducation.com/student/news/student-experience-survey-2017-results

Usher, Alex. 2014. "The War Between Universities and Disciplines." Higher Education Strategy Associates. 8 October. http://higheredstrategy.com/the-war-between-universities-and-disciplines/

Section IV

The Future of Quality Measurement

Postsecondary Punters: Creating New Platforms for Higher-Education Success

Hamish Coates

Making Better Bets on Tertiary Futures

Postsecondary punters are people who place bets on higher education. Higher education is a huge industry and finance firms around the world are active in many investment plays. But most postsecondary punting happens in humble family homes by people wagering that higher education has a part to play in helping them or their loved ones succeed. Improving this kind of punt is essential not just to students and graduates, but more broadly to the industries, organizations, professions, and communities that these people will lead.

As higher education has expanded, so too have widespread calls for information on its value. But there remain core facets of the academy about which very little is known, and available information is often difficult even for specialists to interpret. Traditional disclosure arrangements evolved for highly regulated and supply-driven forms of provision. Recent shifts to far larger and more competitive contexts require radically new disclosures. To guide and sustain future growth, more must be done to report and affirm the sector's value and contribution. It is really important that people have access to insights that sustain confidence and support. This means moving beyond myths and rituals that may feel ingrained yet fail to prove value, creating new data collections

Assessing Quality in Postsecondary Education: International Perspectives, edited by Harvey P. Weingarten, Martin Hicks, and Amy Kaufman. Montréal and Kingston: McGill-Queen's University Press, Queen's Policy Studies Series. © 2018 The School of Policy Studies, Queen's University at Kingston. All rights reserved.

and reporting mechanisms, and sparking new cycles of contribution and improvement.

This chapter takes stock of contemporary developments, and advances a progressive agenda for academic quality. It asserts that higher education must move beyond seeking asylum through coded opacity that fails to disclose the sector's full brilliance and offerings. How people talk, measure, and report on quality is outdated and has done little to make an inquiring public or government more informed, satisfied, or poised to succeed. Major new reporting platforms are required to clarify and prove the value of higher education, and improve investments and outcomes.

The following observations are pitched at a general level and necessarily skirt many of the delicacies and complexities of specific fields, institutions, markets, and industries. The analysis is aimed at the "norm core" of higher education rather than any "dragging tail" or the "high-end elite." It focuses on education rather than research functions. There is an overlap between these two facets of academic work, not least in terms of marketing activities, which are touched on below, and the work of a dwindling number of "traditional" academic staff. But the chapter focuses squarely on the business of education. This is foresight rather than historical research. It distills observations about the past, but the focus is on future reforms rather than past shortcomings.

Buying Higher Education

Delving a little bit into the buying process spurs the simple and always controversial innovation that this chapter advances. Much has been invested in trying to understand and influence how people buy things. Buying is a complex endeavour, even when it comes to small purchases. While it gets even more complex when the thing being consumed is higher education, there appear to be a few fundamental processes at play. Basically, buying involves awareness, searching, deciding, and purchasing (Engel, Kollat, and Blackwell 1968). The first two of these processes are of immediate relevance to this analysis.

Becoming aware of a need or want is an obvious initial step in buying. The formation of such awareness is a complex matter in its own right, which may not be rational, obvious, or sequential. Research into higher-education consumption suggests that a range of cultural, familial, personal, and educational forces all shape people's decision making (Hossler and Gallagher 1987; Moogan and Baron 2003). But increasingly any fine-grained deliberations appear swamped by much broader socio-economic forces. Demand for higher education continues to grow (OECD 2016; UNESCO 2017). A bachelor's degree is the passport to most forms of professional or even much skilled work and in fast-growing economies the ticket to the middle class. The value of such credentials is expanding as economies mature. The growing scale of higher education underlines the importance of getting "awareness formation" right—particularly, but not only, for people from countries or communities without traditional access to tertiary education opportunities.

Second, awareness of the need for a service like higher education launches a search process that identifies options and, for each option, salient parameters and attributes. So, what are the options or the various higher-education services on offer? Next, how should these options be evaluated and what parameters are relevant to consider? Then, what information on each of the parameters is helpful when making a decision? Expertly run procurements might unfold in such sequence, but in practice such searches are likely scatty, sub-rational, and non-articulated. It is also unfair to frame potential higher-education consumers as experts. Most are first-time buyers. Given the demography of the world's high-growth markets, most aspirant consumers have very little personal experience of the industry. And this is an area in which even industry experts can be flummoxed. It is sometimes asserted that education—like eating—is a credence good. There is a need to carefully frame the information that plays into people's deliberations about buying higher education.

These brief forays affirm the great significance of always seeking to do better in making people aware of higher education, and in improving the information that can help people with buying. These are important matters for people and their communities, and the price of failure is high. It is impossible to be too deterministic about education where experience matters as much as substance, but evidence shows (e.g., Taylor, Fry, and Oates 2014) that people are better off if they have the opportunity to participate in higher education, and surely economies benefit most when the most interested and able people are schooled into professions. Both areas canvassed above matter—sparking interest in participation and optimizing the matching of people to courses of study. The two areas are surely interrelated, but this chapter looks specifically into the second—the nature and disclosure of information about higher education.

Craving Confidence

Much has been done over the last three decades to help people buy higher education and afford confidence in the decision they have made. For instance, there have been greater financial disclosures, innumerable policy reviews, billions spent on consultants, ramped-up media attention, more public-spirited academic reporting, the creation of various advisory and information networks, and expanded personnel training. Yet, to date, such efforts have proved inadequate. The "quality movement" provides an interesting case study of the shortcomings of such attempts, and one which links this chapter with the broader book.

In advanced economies, the "quality period" started in the 1990s as higher education expanded beyond elite preserves. Governments sought assurance that public funds were being administered to deliver education of sufficient quality for their growing populations. Quality is a pervasive and expansive idea that touches every facet of university life in different and changing ways. The dominant focus during this period was mainly concerned with educational and administrative functions rather than research or broader engagement. The main approach might be characterized as internal self-evaluation followed by external peer review, the latter being facilitated by some form of quality agency. These agencies were set up by governments and had a reasonably close relationship with universities. Several chapters in Hazelkorn, Coates, and McCormick (2017b) provide a comprehensive analysis of the quality agenda.

This quality-related work achieved much. For instance, it helped build academic management systems within institutions, create large volumes of enhancement-focused R&D, ensure institutions were leading academic matters in ways "fit for purpose," create system-wide and international alignments, and create sector-specific infrastructure and discourse. In essence, the quality period helped professionalize and safeguard higher education.

But in recent times, this prevailing approach to quality has lost its dominant position and increasingly much of its shine. Quality agencies in several countries including the United Kingdom and Australia have been closed, with similar agencies in the United States seemingly bursting at their existential seams (Coates 2017b). The focus on peer review led to variation in the definition and application of standards and overuse of the word "appropriate" to avoid terminal relativism. The focus on institution-level processes yielded diminishing returns and failed to account for the outcomes that really matter. The production of (undoubtedly heavily redacted) industry-centric reports failed to yield information for broader stakeholders, particularly of the kind increasingly viewed as normal in broadband-enhanced societies. The "insider" perspective evolved from collegial arrangements and stumbled seriously in more competitive and commercial settings including with emerging for-profit and private forms of provision. The quality agencies set up to run the processes typically had no, or weak, regulatory powers to enforce any identified improvements. In general, the "quality period" might be seen as setting the foundation for shepherding higher-education institutions in advanced economies from elite to mass scale (Hazelkorn, Coates, and McCormick 2017a). More is required to guide progress in more universal, competitive, and complex times.

Shortcomings in the higher-education sector's own quality agenda fuelled anxieties, particularly among those outside "the university club," which spurred workarounds and new solutions. As the dominant funders of higher education, governments clarified and strengthened their regulatory powers. Consumers sought information from new market-targeted reports on institution performance and, in particular, on research and reputational rankings. New market entrants, in particular for-profit private institutions, used commercial research to strengthen their market plays. Business and community stakeholders continued to flounder in exasperation at the accidental ways they remained forced to engage with higher-education institutions. Of course, separate accreditation exists for certain "professional" fields, though this is not without its own complexities. As even this brief summary conveys, there has been a proliferation of bewildering information about many facets of higher education. This unravelling has ignited confusion, not clarity. No solution thus far has yet addressed the aching need for more effective, sophisticated, and comprehensive disclosures that help people make informed decisions about their initial and ongoing engagement with higher education.

Revealing Success

Next generation reports are needed to help people engage successfully with higher education. A first key step in this quest to provide better information on higher education is identifying what information should be reported. A suite of "success indicators" could yield powerful information on how higher education can help people and communities succeed. To venture in this direction, research was conducted in Australia in 2015–16 to shed light on the nature of success in higher education, and how success might be measured. As detailed by Coates et al. (2016, 2017), the study brought together researchers from eight universities and was overseen by an international advisory group. It entailed a systematic review of educational and psychological literature, procured extensive feedback from thirty-one tertiary institutions, conducted six in-depth institutional site visits and case studies, interviewed a diverse group of forty-four students, and consulted with hundreds of researchers and practitioners in dozens of countries. The research builds on the findings and limitations of a large body of prior work on how students prosper in higher education (e.g., Bice and Coates 2016; Coates and Richardson 2012; Coates 2017a, 2017c; Radloff et al. 2012).

The study defined a new model that deconstructed student success into nine qualities. Table 10.1 presents the nine qualities and shows how they are divided into three broader groups. In articulating these nine qualities it is not assumed that they are exhaustive, incontestable, or mutually exclusive. The terrain is too complex and dynamic for any such claims to be made. Rather, it is contended that the qualities mark out a suite of worthy agendas and carry the potential to create discourse that helps students and their institutions succeed.

Importantly, as the above presentation reveals, the qualities step beyond prevailing terms used to define and operationalize student experience and related constructs. For instance, while "student satisfaction" has become somewhat entrenched, there is ample evidence that beyond stamping out woeful practice, it offers substantially diminishing returns to improving higher education. Worse, it sucks energy and attention away from things that really count as articulated in the nine qualities above. Ingrained phrases such as "teaching quality" and "student support" and "student services" are becoming less relevant as team-based computer-mediated teaching and facilitation becomes more widespread, as evidenced by the near-universal adoption of learning-management and other enterprise-learning systems. The nine qualities are broader than the frequently espoused though rarely measured "graduate attributes." Rather than fixate on what are really supply-centric concepts, they instead project qualities that signal new co-created conceptualizations of higher education.

The qualities are designed to be equally meaningful to diverse stakeholders, including those who haven't thought about higher education, prospective students, students, graduates, employers, teachers, and

Table 10.1

Nine Qualities of a Successful Student Experience

Group	Quality	Description
Student Outcomes	Discovery	Opportunity to discover and create new ideas. Cognitive experience that is motivated intrinsically but mediated socially. Includes research, identification of new, transferable ways of thinking, building emotional capability, and creating social networks.
	Achievement	Attaining sought-after outcomes, including near-term benchmarks (grades, honours, awards), and longer-term completion and attainment goals (getting a good job).
	Connection	Making connections between ideas, people, and experiences. Establishing networks within (student activities) and outside (interest groups, academic exchanges) the institution. Building sensitivity to cultural differences and collaborating with communities, socially and professionally.
	Opportunity	Academic and professional opportunities gained through social connection, provision of insights into prospects, and sense of enrichment and empowerment.
Student Formations	Value	Return on investment. Seeing that higher education is worth the time, cost, and effort. Includes monetary and opportunity costs, as well as broader forms of cognitive and emotional effort and returns.
	Belonging	Being part of something larger than oneself. Aspects of engagement (participation in educationally purposeful activities), but also inclusion in, and recognition of, the individual by the community.
	Identity	Ability to change and define oneself in localized or more expansive ways. Identification with peer groups and increasingly disciplinary or professional identities on the way to becoming a member of civic and professional communities.

Table 10.1, continued

Nine Qualities of a Successful Student Experience

Group	Quality	Description
Student Supports	Enabled	Providing students with new competencies and broader self-regulatory and metacognitive capacities required for thriving in future settings. Based on both learning and leadership experiences within educational settings (classroom, online) and student communities.
	Personalized	Support and guidance received as appropriate to individual needs and when needed (just-in-time, just-enough, and just-for-me). Curricular structures are present, but nimble enough to respond to different individual circumstances.

Source: Borden and Coates (2017)

support staff. Given the transparencies and efficiencies afforded by new technologies and knowledge, it makes little sense to design ideas about education or quality for segmented or partitioned audiences, as has been the case in the past. Instead, as emphasized below, nuanced information can be provided to myriad stakeholders. What this means in concrete terms is that the same data in aggregated form could flow through to academic leaders and used to produce personalized reports for individuals.

To guide individual success, it is necessary to chart paths through each of the nine qualities. This involves identifying thresholds of increasing success for each quality. This does not imply that every student proceeds stepwise or even necessarily through each threshold, or that each threshold is meaningful for each student. It does imply a fundamental structure that underpins each quality and is relatively invariant across environments and people. This is uncontroversial if the thresholds are defined in sufficiently general ways and are able through the process of measurement to be particularized in relevant and helpful ways. It is also necessary to deploy technology for modelling individual profiles and journeys. Simply put, a profile can be envisaged as a complex dynamic of diverse attributes that portray an individual in relation to a successful student experience. A journey is a multiple-branching pathway through a higher-education process, from beginning to end.

The idea of profiling "movements through journeys" steps well beyond the idea of shifting "batched groups through life cycles." Together these two approaches may seem at first glance to unleash infinite complexity for conceptualizing and managing each student's experience, but experience in other industries implies otherwise. After initial reworking in terms of new processes, effective digitization has been shown to yield substantial increases in productivity and quality of people's purposeful interactions with organizations.

As part of the Australian foundation project, initial efforts were made to identify sources of robust data to measure each of the nine qualities, or at least prove the feasibility of their measurement. Table 10.2 demonstrates that a range of collection techniques and data sources are needed. The examples are rooted in the Australian context but are sufficiently broad to support generalization to other settings.

Next Generation Platforms

New platforms are required to report information in ways that help people succeed. Having the right information is necessary, but not sufficient for improving how people buy higher education. Information already abounds in higher education, though as identified above, there is substantial scope for repackaging it. Better reporting is also required.

What are the problems with current platforms? There are many, and the following high-level synthesis of the shortcomings of this young and fast-growing field is not intended to be expansive, conclusive, or focus on any initiative in particular. In summary, it is not uncommon for reports to present highly diffuse information on a narrow range of institutional (mostly research) functions that is lagged, sourced from third parties, often annual, and of unverified or unknown validity and reliability. Such information is often presented online in static ordinal lists without regard to interpretation or consequence. Reports may be provided without full disclosure of political or commercial interests or intentions. The current reporting landscape is just too confusing, even for experts, but especially for punters.

Coates (2017b) clarified how reports must improve as part of a comprehensive analysis of transparency in higher education. In summary, future reports must become more comprehensive, more sophisticated, and more effective. Exploration of each of these dimensions charts substantial opportunities to innovate in this growing field.

Reporting platforms need to broaden to include more information of

... continued on page 187

Table 10.2

Data Sources for the Nine Qualities

Quality	Associated Indicators	Data Availability
Discovery	Development of new technical, generic, and personal skills; advanced problem-solving skills, production of a body of creative academic work; understanding academic culture and expectations; and acquisition of new interests	Lagged data is available from national student and graduate surveys. There is a shortage of collected data that measures students' capacity for discovery; however, internal data points including curriculum and assessment systems, and commercial online profiling platforms would yield richer information.
Achievement	Admission, passing, retention, learning outcomes, completion, and articulation into other qualifications	Lagged data is available from national student surveys, data collections, and state-based admissions agencies. Additional information could be harnessed through e-portfolios or tracking mechanisms. There is a shortage of publicly available information on learning outcomes.
Opportunity	Awareness of career opportunities and strategies, further study readiness, graduate employment, participating in collaborative networks, and participating in experiential learning or in leadership roles	Lagged data is available from national student, graduate, and employer surveys. Additional information could be gained from admission agencies and institutional alumni information and systems. There is a shortage of collected data that measures opportunities seized by individual students; however, participation in institutional events, leadership roles, experiential activities, and graduate outcomes could be logged.

Table 10.2, continued

Data Sources for the Nine Qualities

Quality	Associated Indicators	Data Availability
Value	Graduate outcomes, course fees, course duration, work experience opportunities, physical and online facilities and services, perceptions of teacher quality, identification of study purpose aspirations, and student information	Lagged data is available from national student, graduate, and employer surveys. Additional information could be gained from student service use and incidence of attendance, exit interviews, institutional alumni systems, and social media platforms.
Connection	Exposure to industry events, speakers, and networks; undertaking work placements; student exchange and volunteering; and forming academic, collegial, and social networks	Lagged data is available from national student surveys. Additional information could be gained from institutional systems, work-integrated learning experiences, online discussion boards, interaction in student groups, commercial networks used in coursework, and new collections that log student attendance or participation in industry or academic events. Subscriptions, membership, and participation in professional or academic networking platforms, organizations, and chat rooms would indicate connectedness.
Belonging	Feeling welcome; awareness and participation in groups, forums, and clubs; participation in online and face-to-face curricular and non-curricular activities; and forming and maintaining relationships	Lagged data is available from national student and graduate surveys. Additional institutional systems that log participation, attendance, and duration of experience on campus or online could be used in conjunction with records that indicate attendance at orientation events, membership, and participation in groups. Other new forms of data could include real-time student feedback about perceptions or swipe-card data. Alumni information and commercial online profiling offer other data.

Table 10.2, continued

Data Sources for the Nine Qualities

Quality	Associated Indicators	Data Availability
Personalized	Staff engagement with students, tailoring curriculum and teaching to students, experience/advice that is tailored to individuals, and provision of real-time assessment	Data is available, or could be made available, from national student surveys and institutional systems on the extent to which staff and infrastructure are personalized. There is more information available on commercial platforms.
Enabled	Student aid, scholarship availability, teacher quality, assessment feedback, academic support, online and physical resources, and student development sessions	Lagged data is available from national student and graduate surveys. Information from tertiary admission centres, and institutional scholarship data could be used. Additional institutional systems that record use of support services, attendance at non-compulsory curricular events, use of online and physical resources including career advice or utilization of digital systems would provide information. Institutional information about alumni and commercial online profiling offer other data.
Identity	Leadership skills, cultural awareness, emotional intelligence, self-reflectiveness	Lagged data is available from national student and graduate surveys. Institutional systems are those that house administrative data and assessment items including reflective and practical journals, capstone experiences, and exchanges. Data identifies participation in mentoring, leadership, orientation events, or peer-assisted programs. Information about student awards and recognition, and volunteer roles for both curricular and non-curricular activities could be captured. Other commercial online systems or personal blogs offer additional data.

Source: Coates et al. (2017)

direct relevance to how prospective and current learners engage with higher education. While information on research conveys status, drives brand, spurs buying behaviour, and is attractive to institution executives, it leads to myriad distortions. Individuals seek to study at institutions because of research endeavours that have nothing, besides perhaps credential brand, to do with their education. Institutions, for their part, seek to do "world-class research" even if it is beyond their reach. Nations aspire for all institutions to pursue global research rather than serve more diverse local needs. Rather than emphasize research, platforms should report the kind of successful qualities articulated earlier in this chapter.

Reports need to become more sophisticated. They must move from being static, to being dynamic, and even personalized. As computing technologies have advanced, there has been a notable shift toward more dynamic, online-rating systems. Rather than disseminate static information, reporting agencies have developed more nuanced means for engaging with information about higher-education activity and performance. But increasingly, reporting mechanisms are becoming more personalized. Generic internet search engines are perhaps the most flexible means of sourcing information about higher education, though the lack of guiding structure is confusing. Social-networking platforms are an evidently important source of information for stakeholders, as are individual institution websites. As well, a range of other independent platforms are emerging that enable individuals to select from specified criteria to generate customized comparisons of institutions and programs of study.

Reports on higher education must become more effective, shifting well beyond the anarchy that currently prevails. Drawing from broader governance settings, Coates (2017b) identified that reports must be robust and assured, relevant and accessible, timely and ongoing, intentional and engaging, and regulated and accountable. In a nutshell, information must be robust and assured such that only quality information is reported. Information must be disclosed in ways that are relevant and accessible to target audiences. It is essential that disclosures about higher-education activity and performance are timely and continuous. Public institutions should be intentional and engaging in their reporting practices. It is important that there are effective means of governing overall reporting arrangements, particularly in expanding and anarchical environments.

Indeed, in recent decades there has been a general progression in each of these three areas. Scott (2013) has clarified that the 1990s saw the emergence of "first-generation" reports that were distributed via static print, presenting heavily lagged and partial data of varying quality sourced from compliance reports. The 2000s saw the rise of more efficacious "second-generation" reports of greater scope and increasing sophistication. Examples include the current international rankings and a host of national initiatives (Hazelkorn 2010). The 2010s saw the rise of more effective "third-generation" transparency mechanisms that can be nuanced toward individual preferences and encompass a greater range of functions. Such reports have proliferated as demand for information has intensified.

A core thrust of the current argument is to spur creation of the "next-generation" or "fourth-generation" suite of reports, delivering information that is more dynamic and hopefully more robust. These reports should unfold at two parallel levels of analysis: institution- or program-level benchmarking tools for industry insiders like ministries and institutions, and nuanced platforms particularized to the interests of individuals seeking to engage in higher education. Given the transparencies and efficiencies afforded by new technologies, it makes little sense to continue designing ideas about education or quality for segmented or partitioned audiences. Next- or fourth-generation reports may be designed to communicate equally meaningfully to diverse stakeholders, including people who haven't thought about higher education, prospective students, students, graduates, employers, teachers, and support staff. In concrete terms, this means the same data in aggregated form could flow through to academic leaders as is used to produce personalized reports for individuals.

As with advisory platforms in any area of life, next generation reports should join what people get from higher education with what they initially invest. The platforms should articulate and align what people bring to higher education, the experiences they seek, and the success that they want. Such platforms carry the potential to dynamically clarify rather than compartmentalize options, experiences, and outcomes. They are unlikely to "solve" all problems with buying higher education, but would likely play a direct part in improving choices, progress, and outcomes for universities, students, professions, and communities. More broadly, insights could be used by universities to improve the engagement, contribution, and success of their students and graduates.

Where to Next?

Sprung from the simple proposition that there is ample opportunity to improve how people punt with higher education, this chapter has charted the need for, and nature of, new reporting platforms. It looked at weaknesses in how people buy higher education, shortcomings of current quality arrangements, the need for information to help students succeed, and finally, the impetus for new reporting platforms. It has been argued that in the future, higher education must be unrecognizably more transparent. There is a need to improve the nature and governance of disclosures, a need for more information, a need for a shift in focus from inputs and processes to outcomes, impact, and value or success, and a need for more effective reporting platforms.

Of course, as in any large-scale context, the field's development will be patterned by a range of forces. Several hurdles exist. Established international rankings are supported by power dynamics that underpin reputation and prestige. Many of the particularly prominent reporting initiatives have also secured a first-mover advantage through being early entrants in this young field. Indicator definition and data collection have proved troublesome and costly, particularly for education and engagement functions. Establishing that data is robust on a broad scale is always challenging, but there is substantial room to align ranking techniques with expected standards in international comparative evaluation. A range of facilitators, including public expectations, will undoubtedly fuel greater disclosure.

What, then, would be the characteristics of a helpful way forward? Essentially, there appears to be value in advancing some kind of non-profit and likely non-governmental initiative. The need for a non-profit approach is critical to steer clear of any commercial sensitivities or conflicts of interest. A non-governmental approach is needed to engage higher-education institutions and other stakeholder agencies on equal footing, recognizing, of course, that governments fund most higher education and spark many important initiatives. An appropriate series of governance, leadership, and management arrangements would need to be formed. These arrangements must be multi-stakeholder in nature. They must go well beyond engaging sector insiders alone and give equal power to other higher-education stakeholders. The initiative will be inherently international, which is essential given that higher education is marking out a new series of borderless arrangements that transcend existing agreements and dialogues. A charter with guiding principles and policies should be developed that speaks to the espoused technical principles, and guides the conduct of the initiative. The spark for such development will almost surely arise from conversations and debates among existing stakeholders, early adopters and advocates, though a medium- to long-term view will be required. As with the development of any new field, there is a need to define and position such interests.

As flagged throughout this chapter, new value is being created by new contributors, evolving technologies, and changes to higher education itself. Reporting is a young field and there are substantial opportunities for innovation. While work has commenced on many of the areas mentioned, it is difficult to forecast when new indicators and data sources will become available. If past progress is any guide, it would seem reasonable to envisage change over the next five to ten years. This is an area of substantial opportunities for growth.

References

Bice, Sara, and Hamish Coates. 2016. "University Sustainability Reporting: Taking Stock of Transparency." *Tertiary Education and Management* 22 (1): 1–18.

Borden, Victor M. H., and Hamish Coates. 2017. "Learning Analytics as a Counterpart to Surveys of Student Experience." *New Directions for Higher Education* 2017 (179): 89–102. doi:10.1002/he.20246

Coates, Hamish. 2017a. "Development of the Field and Formation of More Consolidated Perspectives." In *Assessment of Learning Outcomes in Higher Education—Cross National Comparisons and Perspectives*, edited by Olga Zlatkin-Troitschanskaia, Hans Anand Pant, Miriam Toepper, Corinna Lautenbach, and Christiane Kuhn. Dordrecht: Springer.

———. 2017b. *The Market for Learning: Leading Transparent Higher Education*. Dordrecht: Springer.

———, ed. 2017c. *Productivity in Higher Education: Research Insights for Universities and Governments in Asia*. Tokyo: Asian Productivity Organization.

Coates, Hamish, Paula Kelly, Ryan Naylor, and Victor Borden. 2016. "Innovative Approaches for Enhancing the 21st Century Student Experience." *Alternation* 23 (1): 62–89.

———. 2017. *Innovative Approaches for Enhancing the 21st Century Student Experience*. Canberra: Department of Education and Training.

Coates, Hamish, and Sarah Richardson. 2012. "An International Assessment of Bachelor Degree Graduates' Learning Outcomes." *Higher Ed-*

ucation Management and Policy 23 (3), 51–69. https://doi.org/10.1787/hemp-23-5k9h5xkx575c

Engel, James F., David T. Kollat, and Roger D. Blackwell. 1968. *Consumer Behaviour*. New York: Holt, Rinehart and Winston.

Hazelkorn, Ellen. 2010. *Are Rankings a Useful Transparency Instrument?* Presented at the Meeting of the Directors General of Higher Education, Namur, 13 September. http://media.ehea.info/file/Transparency_Namur_September_2010/92/1/Are_Rankings_a_Useful_Transparency_599921.pdf

Hazelkorn, Ellen, Hamish Coates, and Alexander McCormick. 2017a. "Quality, Performance, and Accountability: Emergent Challenges in the Global Era." In *Handbook on Quality, Performance and Accountability*, edited by Ellen Hazelkorn, Hamish Coates, and Alexander McCormick. Cheltenham: Edward Elgar.

———, eds. 2017b. *Handbook on Quality, Performance and Accountability*. Cheltenham: Edward Elgar.

Hossler, Don, and Karen S. Gallagher. 1987. "Studying Student College Choice: A Three-Phase Model and the Implications for Policymakers." *College and University* 62 (3): 207–21.

Moogan, Yvonne J., and Sherry Baron. 2003. "An Analysis of Student Characteristics Within the Student Decision Making Process." *Journal of Further and Higher Education* 27 (3): 271–87.

OECD (Organisation for Economic Co-operation and Development). 2016. *Education at a Glance 2016: OECD indicators*. Paris: OECD Publishing.

Radloff, A., Hamish Coates, R. James, and K. Krause. 2012. *Development of the University Experience Survey (UES)*. Canberra: Department of Education, Employment and Workplace Relations.

Scott, Peter. 2013. "Ranking Higher Education Institutions: A Critical Perspective." In *Rankings and Accountability in Higher Education: Uses and Misuses*, edited by Priscilla T. M. Marope, Peter J. Wells, and Ellen Hazelkorn. 113–27. Paris: UNESCO Publishing.

Taylor, Paul, Rick Fry, and Russ Oates. 2014. *The Rising Cost of Not Going to College*. Washington: Pew Research Center.

UNESCO Institute for Statistics. 2017. *Higher Education*. http://uis.unesco.org/en/topic/higher-education

Conclusion

Harvey P. Weingarten, Martin Hicks, and Amy Kaufman

As evident from the preceding chapters, participants in our workshop provided sharply divergent approaches and opinions about how to measure academic quality. We expected no less, given the global slate of participants we assembled for this initiative. Yet, even though the contributors work in distinct contexts, jurisdictions, and systems, common themes and issues emerged from our conversations about approaches to quality measurement.

If there was one shared call to action, it was that we do not yet do as good a job as we should of measuring academic quality. As Hamish Coates points out in the final chapter, doing better is essential not only for students and their families, but also for the industries, organizations, professions, and communities that our graduates will one day lead. Figuring out how to do a better job is what the workshop and this book are about.

We extracted four important overarching messages from the presentations that have informed our own thinking about this issue.

1. A Role for Government

In many of the examples presented in this publication, the measurement of academic quality was motivated by government attempts to evaluate the performance and value of postsecondary systems. The examples from the Netherlands, UK, Nova Scotia, and Ireland provide prime examples. In most of these cases, there was an underlying sentiment that initiatives to transparently measure academic quality had not (and perhaps never would) arise organically from the higher-education institutions themselves.

2. Two Approaches to Measuring Quality

The second key takeaway from this project is related to the chosen measurement approach, the dynamics of which depend greatly on who is driving the initiative and the intended purpose of the selected measurements. Two dominant approaches and purposes were evident. The first, as noted above, is driven by government and its desire to assess the value or impact of its investment in postsecondary institutions. These schemes are largely motivated by government's attempts to hold institutions accountable.

The second is driven by the desire of institutions to measure the quality of their programs and of student learning outcomes, and to improve them. For the latter group, faculty buy-in is essential. For the former, not so much.

The timeframe for addressing the measurement challenge also varies between the two. Governments are impatient for a measurement scheme, believing that it is better to have indicators of academic quality available immediately, even though they may be imperfect or indirect. Institutions are prepared to move more slowly in an effort to refine indicators, assess their reliability and validity, and secure community buy-in prior to their release. Cynics may argue that these behaviours reflect a motivation to slow down the measurement initiative as much as possible.

3. Little Evidence of Impact

One of the goals of the workshop was to obtain evidence of the degree to which measurement efforts influence program development, curricula, and resource allocation by government or institutions—regardless of the perspective or strategy adopted to measure quality. We were looking for evidence that the efforts that have gone into these quality-measurement processes are having an impact. We were underwhelmed by the evidence. We need a better way of linking measurement efforts to institutional changes and decisions to improve academic programming and outcomes for students. While our participants readily agreed that this is an important loop that needs to close, figuring out how to do it proves difficult. The case for the importance of tying performance measurements to actual action was made most strongly in the chapter by Alexander McCormick and Jillian Kinzie.

4. Beware the Unintended Consequences

Participants were keenly sensitive to two principles: what you measure matters, and it's possible, and perhaps even natural, to game a poorly constructed measurement system. We heard many cautionary statements about how measurement systems could undermine or pervert academic quality. For example, using graduation rates as a surrogate measure for quality might lead institutions to lower standards for retention and graduation, or diminish equity of access by enrolling only those students who are sure to succeed. For us this underscored the importance of developing a measurement system that gauges directly what students learn (the chapter by Roger Benjamin provides a good example). At a minimum, the measurement system must identify teaching practices that research has shown lead to improved learning, much like the indicators proposed by Aaron Horn and David Tandberg.

Where Do We Go from Here?

One of HEQCO's goals in organizing this workshop was to get the best advice from experts about how we can weave the measurement of academic quality into our mandated task of measuring the performance of Ontario's postsecondary system. We have taken away the following lessons.

First, given our legislated mandate, the primary requirement for HEQCO is to provide the best possible advice to government to help improve its postsecondary system. Therefore, our task is to develop a set of indicators that will assess the impact of government policies (such as a new postsecondary funding formula or reforms to the province's student financial-aid system) on the quality of Ontario's postsecondary system. These indicators will be useful to institutions too, but the primary emphasis should be on indicators that are useful to government and the system as a whole.

Second, the purpose of quality measurement should be the improvement of the postsecondary system. We are not inclined to select indicators for the purpose of ranking institutions, or simply to demonstrate accountability. The government and institutions need to be able to monitor the quality of the academic experience they offer students so they can engage in a process of continuous improvement. We must make it difficult for government or other organizations to use them otherwise.

Third, if the indicators are to be useful to those within government and within institutions who have the power to drive improvement, then they must be tangible, easy to understand, and limited in number to capture a true sense of achievable priorities.

Fourth, indicators must be designed or used in a way that respects the diversity of the higher-education institutions within the system. Institutions differ greatly in terms of their mandates and the student populations they enrol. Indicators that do not accommodate these differing realities or missions would be open to misinterpretation or lead to suboptimal outcomes.

Finally, our concerns about proxy or surrogate measures of learning have been strongly reinforced by this project. They are too easily gamed because they largely miss the very point they are trying to measure. Rather, we are predisposed to measures that are reflective of student learning, preferably direct measures of learning itself. Again, Roger Benjamin effectively makes the case for the assessment of generic skills, which he argues can be both assessed and improved by teaching. And if the direct measurement of learning is not yet possible, and we are forced to rely on measurements of processes that drive academic quality, then what we measure has to be as close as possible to learning itself. The chapter by McCormick and Kinzie provides examples of this thinking.

We offer an example from HEQCO's current work. HEQCO is conducting a trial to measure changes in the literacy, numeracy, and problem-solving skills of Ontario's postsecondary students from the time they start their programs to when they finish. Virtually all higher-education leaders claim that students who attend their institutions will be more literate, numerate, and better problem solvers as a result of their postsecondary programs. Our trial, called the Essential Adult Skills Initiative (EASI), involves eleven colleges and nine universities, and uses a psychometrically reliable and valid measure of these skills to document the changes between entering and graduating students. In our view, this is a direct measurement of learning and is measured in a way that takes into account the diversity of the student populations in different institutions.

The Evolution of Quality Measures

Those interested in better measures of academic quality should be encouraged by reading the views, perspectives, and data presented in these chapters. We are moving from a world where academic quality is simply taken for granted to one where actual measures of quality are gaining acceptance. Measurement must be the foundation of improving the academic programs we offer. Is it simple? No. Do we have all of the instruments we need to construct and learn from reliable and valid measures of academic quality? Not yet, but we have some. Can we know for sure how these measurements will be used, by whom, and to what end? Not necessarily. But we do know that measuring academic quality is important—as important as the effort we put into measuring research quality, which is done routinely even though such measures are acknowledged to be imperfect. And we know what questions we need to ask to do a good job of measuring quality, no matter how difficult, anxiety-provoking, and challenging. Ultimately, it is an essential exercise for the advancement of a robust economy, a vibrant society, and a better quality of life. We hope this book helps those thinking through the problem. It has helped us.

In the spirit of improvement, we have already begun to integrate what we have learned into the evolution of our performance measurement design thinking in Ontario. We propose a focused set of performance indicators designed to assist our primary audience—government—achieve its key priorities for the higher-education system. They are improving academic quality through the direct measurement of learning (reflecting what we have learned from this project), achieving equity of access for underrepresented Ontarians, and maintaining institutional sustainability.

Finally, we wish to express our deep gratitude to our contributors, all of whom are thoughtful, creative, and committed to the goal of measuring quality in higher education. They generously gave their time at the workshop and in the ensuing to and fro while chapters were reviewed. As we had hoped, we learned a great deal from their work, expertise, and experiences.